THE HEALING POWER OF COMBINING HANDS ON HEALING WITH ANGELIC ENERGY AND AROMATHERAPY

DISCOVER THE HISTORY OF ENERGY HEALING AND LEARN HOW TO USE YOUR HANDS TO HEAL

ANTONIA (TONI) BRASTED, PHD, CGC, RA

BALBOA.PRESS
A DIVISION OF HAY HOUSE

Balboa Press books may be ordered through booksellers or by contacting:

Balboa Press
A Division of Hay House
1663 Liberty Drive
Bloomington, IN 47403
www.balboapress.com
844-682-1282

Because of the dynamic nature of the Internet, any web addresses or links contained in this book may have changed since publication and may no longer be valid. The views expressed in this work are solely those of the author and do not necessarily reflect the views of the publisher, and the publisher hereby disclaims any responsibility for them.

The author of this book does not dispense medical advice or prescribe the use of any technique as a form of treatment for physical, emotional, or medical problems without the advice of a physician, either directly or indirectly. The intent of the author is only to offer information of a general nature to help you in your quest for emotional and spiritual well-being. In the event you use any of the information in this book for yourself, which is your constitutional right, the author and the publisher assume no responsibility for your actions.

Any people depicted in stock imagery provided by Getty Images are models, and such images are being used for illustrative purposes only.
Certain stock imagery © Getty Images.

Print information available on the last page.

ISBN: 979-8-7652-3560-7 (sc)
ISBN: 979-8-7652-3562-1 (hc)
ISBN: 979-8-7652-3561-4 (e)

Library of Congress Control Number: 2022919042

Balboa Press rev. date: 10/19/2022

CONTENTS

PART II

PREFACE

The future of healing energy research.

In the twentieth-century, we have begun to explore a *universal model,* based upon Einsteinian relativity: a complex and interconnected universe of particle and energy fields, in which matter and energy are interconvertible. We are finally coming to accept the *probability* that universal systems are interactive, and that we, human beings, are an integral part of these systems—and of the *whole.*

Recently, in a lecture for the International Society for the Study of Subtle Energies and Energy Medicine, Dr. Larry Dossey recounted an old story that is a metaphor for man's progress toward understanding universal laws:

"There was once an argument among the gods over where to hide the secret of life so that men and women would not find it. One god said: Bury it under a mountain; they will never look there. No, the others said, one day they will find ways to dig up mountains and will uncover it. Another said: Sink it in the depths of the ocean; it will be safe there. No the others objected, humans will one day find a way to plumb the ocean's depths and find it easily. Finally another god said: Put it inside them; men and women will never think of looking for it there. All the gods agreed, and so that is how the secret of life came to be hidden within us."

I believe that we are now approaching the time when we will finally unlock our inner wisdom, learns to look inside of ourselves for the secret of life, and therefore honor our interconnectedness to everything in the universe. We will then understand our influence on all persons and things around us. We will become aware that our emotions and thoughts play a *major role* in our physical health. *Energy healing* will then cease to be considered *paranormal;* rather, we will come to *re-discover* an ancient wisdom: the truly *effective* way to treat physical illness is through comprehension of the human being as a whole.

ACKNOWLEDGEMENTS

I would like to take this opportunity to express my heartfelt gratitude to my teacher, Stevan Thayer, the developer of Integrated Energy Therapy – IET. Stevan's support inspiration and assistance on many levels were primordial to developing my confidence and trust in my channeling and healing capabilities. Also, I extend my gratitude to my teachers Sanaya Roman and Duane Packer, and to their spiritual guides, Orin and Daben, for teaching me how to awaken my light body. Their classes and books have been my sustaining source of strength during times of great personal difficulty.

I also would like to show appreciation and gratitude to all the healers and writers that are part of the bibliography on this book, it was thanks to their work that I was able to educate myself and collect material to now share with others.

Above all others, I thank you, Ariel, my guide and guardian angel, whose presence has been so constant in my life. Your patience and forgiveness of my many shortcomings is an inspiring example of unconditional love.

INTRODUCTION

*... "they shall lay hands-on the sick, and they shall recover. " - (KJV) Mark 16:18
... "anointed many sick people with oil and healed them", - Mark 6:13*

Hopefully this book will be a humble reminder to all of those involved in healing work, which combines two healing techniques that are as powerful today as they were in the Biblical times.

Anointing with essential oil was commonly practiced throughout the Scriptures for many different purposes. The New Testament mentions it specifically in connection with praying for the sick.

Today's Aromatherapy is practiced in many different settings and variations, but a common denominator among all aroma therapists is the sense of reverence towards the miracle of nature in the form of essential oils. They know that fragrance can affect the mood, calm, relax and release emotions.

Today's energy work also comes in a variety of methods, but what all of them have in common is the unconditional love and the spiritual meaning of healing. Any energy work practitioner knows that to treat "the sick" it is primordial to access the client's mental, emotional and spiritual state. The word "sick" literally means "without strength." This "weakness" covers a whole list of dysfunctions - illness, disease, tiredness, spiritual struggles, depression, resentment, hopelessness, anger and so on.

The challenge until now was how to combine those two healing techniques, in a format that would fit today's reality. Not only would it help professional aroma therapists and energy healers to blend those techniques in their work, but also, would give to the lay people, tools to work on themselves and help their loved ones. I believe this book is the missing link that will prepare the reader to further awake the healer within by combining aromatherapy *and* energy work, to create miracles in the lives they touch.

The first section of this book will give you extended background on energy healing from ancient times to today's methods, and will succinctly describe several energy healing modalities in use today.

The second section of this book will give you a basic knowledge of Aromatherapy and chemistry as well as a description of the correlation of each essential oil with the emotions.

May God bless your work of love and compassionate touching!

BACKGROUND

I was born and raised in São Paulo, Brazil. The death of my father occurred when I was only three years old. His loss prevented my mother from dedicating a lot of time to her five kids. Other than going to Catholic services on Sundays and attending special church services on the holidays, there was seldom talk of religious ideas in my household and consequently, no talk of the interconnections among Body, Mind and Spirit.

Health care was another difficult issue in my household. Being a low-income family with no health insurance, we did not have the luxury to visit a doctor to take care of our health problems, which probably were aggravated by poor nutrition. My first consultation with a doctor was at the age of 13 years: Already working, I could afford to pay my bills. Before the age of 13, however, we were treated by my mother with herbs and homemade remedies.

In my teenager years, I acquired a better understanding of what my mother had done for us. My curiosity about her natural wisdom opened the door for me to acquire self-knowledge and knowledge of other health care modalities besides allopathic medicine. I investigated herbal therapy, aromatherapy and homeopathy. Aromatherapy has been part of my daily life since.

After my father's death, my mother's parents assisted her by offering her a place to live; consequently, from the time that I was three years of age, I spent a great deal of time with my grandparents.

Being very close to my grandfather and filled with a child's curiosity,

I found myself closely observing everything he did. My grandfather claimed to be a gifted healer. Although he had a normal daytime job, after 5:00 p.m. he would tend to a large number of people who came to him for healing a great variety of ailments: maladies ranging from simple toothaches to cancer.

I would often observe his work, not quite understanding his method of healing. He would have the client sit in a chair, close to his home altar. He would then say a prayer while moving both of his hands around the client's body (about one inch away from it). He would finalize the healing by holding his hands over the client's head for a few minutes.

I remember my grandmother becoming upset because of the disturbance that all those people, coming and going, would create in her household. My grandfather would simply respond that there was nothing else that he could do. He felt that healing others was his central mission in life, something that he *had* to do.

He never charged a penny for his work: He believed that he had to give for free that which he gotten for free. He fulfilled his life's mission until the age of 84, when he died from a heart attack.

The time that I spent observing my grandfather's healing work was the motivating force in my personal search for explanations of the unknown: My grandfather was a practicing Roman Catholic who never missed attending a Sunday mass. Hands-on healing, however, was not a regular practice taught by the Catholic Church. Although deeply spiritual, he had no knowledge of spiritualism. Where did he learn his skills? How did he know what to do? Were his curative powers real? If not, why would people come back to him for healing? Is there such a thing as a healing power? If so, where and by what means could one obtain it? Are some persons especially chosen to heal others; or, can anyone heal?

Early in my teen years, my personal search for knowledge, also led me to engage in extensive research on different modalities of healing: Reiki, Therapeutic Touch, Healing with Crystals, Healing through Prayer,

Healing through Meditation, Spiritual Surgery, etc. Although different modalities of healing are practiced in different ways, I came to realize that all forms of healing that I had studied had a central commonality: they *all* work with energy.

It was this latter realization of a central commonality that impelled me to focus my research upon human energy: an understanding of which is prerequisite to understanding how human healing works.

As I dedicated this book to my mother Adelina Gottsfritz and my grandfather, José da Silva Botelho, the two first healers I met in life, who initiated the healing knowledge that I acquired through my life. I have no doubt that their souls are watching over me, guiding my steps along the path to serving others. I pray that each reader will send a thought of light to their soul, healers long overdue for recognition of a lifetime spent in marvelous and unselfish work in serving others.

THE HISTORY OF HANDS-ON HEALING

Laying on of Hands-on of hands, as a form of medicine, dates back at least fifteen-thousand years, to the period when Stone Age artists carved pictographs of healers at work into the walls of Pyrenean caves. Early Egyptian rock carvings and papyrus writing testify to the healing powers of the human touch. Greek mythology tells how Aesculapius not only restored the sick to health by using his *god hand*, but raised the dead as well. And, in the time of Hippocrates, around 400 BC, Greek *cheirourgos* (from whence came the term (surgeon) ministered to the sick, not primarily with scalpels, but with healing palms and fingers.

Among the Romans, the renowned Galleon, physician to the emperor Marcus Aurelio in the second century AD, followed Hippocrate's example by employing gentle massage as a healing method. Various Roman emperors were said to have a strong healing touch. Hadrian was reputedly able to relieve dropsy by a laying on of royal hands, while Vespasian was noted for his cures of neurological disorders, as well as lameness and blindness. In the third century BC, the pagan monarch, King Pyrrhus of Epirus, was famed for curing colic by the laying on not of hands, but of toes. Hands (or toes), the royal healing touch was an apparently divine gift, which would continue through the ages, well into the eighteenth century.

The New Testament describes how Jesus *touched* blind men's eyes (or treated them with his saliva), and restored sight, touched crippled legs, and made them strong again, and touched the heads of madmen, restoring sanity to their minds. Matthew quotes Jesus, specifically instructing the apostles to carry on his work: "Heal the sick, raise the dead, cleanse the lepers, cast out devils." (Matthew 10:8) Following Christ's latter commandment, his disciples regarded their duty to heal the sick essential to preaching the gospel.

The Christian tradition of miraculous cures continued throughout the middle Ages and into the Renaissance. Later Christians—among them Saints Francis, Augustine, Ambrose, Martin, Catherine, Patrick, and Bernard—were renowned for their healing touch. And, like Jesus, the Christian saints ministered to illnesses of the mind, as well as illnesses of the body. Although many historic healers had strong religious ties, others have had few—or no—religious associations, whatsoever.

Robert the Pious of France and Edward the Confessor of England reportedly cured goiter and scrofula (primary tuberculosis of the lymph nodes), by placing their Hands-on the necks of the sick and making the sign of the cross. In earlier times, those who claimed a *divine right* to rule were also credited with a divine power to *heal*. Charles II is reputed to have passed out 90,798 gold coins to the sick. There is some question; however, as to whether Charles donated the coins or sold them to his clients.

History records many commoners also gifted with healing touch. Valentine Greatrakes, a seventh-century Irish landowner and magistrate, practiced a healing technique known as *stroking*. Indeed, Robert Boyle, the founder of modern chemistry, testified to Greatrakes's success. In 1666, Greatrakes embarked on a highly successful tour of London, treating cases of paralysis, deafness, headache, and arthritis—for which he would accept no payment.

In the nineteenth century, interest in spiritualism and the occult was high. Faith healers, such as Andrew Jackson Davis of New York and J. R. Newton of Rhode Island, held mass meetings to demonstrate their skills. They poured hot water over the heads of clients with nervous disorders but opted for a simple lying on of hands to treat tumors or swellings. New England healer Phineas Parkhurst Quimby of Portland, Maine, started out using magnetic sweeps of the body in treating his clients. Later in his practice, Quimby began to suspect that what really cured people was neither divine intervention nor the way he manipulated their animal magnetism; rather, it was how he changed their mental attitudes toward their ailments.

Olga Worrall, well-known twentieth-century healer, was a member of the Methodist laity. Together with her husband, Ambrose, the Worralls began a healing practice in 1950, at Baltimore's Mt. Washington United Methodist Church. Those who had felt Olga Worrall's hands described a powerful sensation of heat infusing their bodies.

New York healer Barbara Ann Brennan claims her roots are in ancient, universal life forces. She describes her technique as "laying-on of hands", that involves re-balancing the Human Energy Field that exists around all of us" (Brennan 1997, 23). Brennan claims to possess what she calls the higher sense perception, which she describes as the ability to read the energy field that surrounds every person. She claims that, by means of meditation, she enters an expanded state of consciousness that enables her to diagram a client's ills. The colors and shapes she sees correspond to the balance of the field. By the laying-on of her hands, combined with higher-sense-perception diagnosis, Brennan believes that she is able to interact with another person's energy field and re-balance it.

In England, a noted hand healer, named Matthew Manning, says that he discovered at an early age that he possessed psychokinetic powers that, he could move objects around simply by willing them do to so. As an adult, he has supposedly channeled his psychokinetic energies into healing with remarkable effect. A client is first asked to describe his or her symptoms. Manning then stands behind the client and places his Hands-on the client's shoulders. His hands begin to move, seemingly of their own volition, seeking out the source of pain—or an organ, perhaps related to the disease. The healing sessions last about thirty minutes; Manning estimates that about two out of every three clients gain relief from their symptoms.

In Russia, a one-time Moscow waitress, named Dzhuna Davitashvili, has won fame by treating clients with a life-giving force called bioenergy. Bioenergy draws on the theories of *prana* and *shi*, those subtle energies of ancient Eastern belief. According to Davitashvili and other Eastern European healers, bioenergy streams forth from the palms of the hands, unblocking and replenishing the depleted energies of the ill. No less a personage than Leonid Brezhnev, whose slurred speech and halting walk marked him as a very sick man in the winter of 1979 is said to have sought treatment at the healing hands of Davitashvili. The following spring, the former Soviet leader showed dramatic improvement. (Apparently Brezhnev's cure was not permanent; he died less than three years later.) With fame came fortune for the onetime waitress, who reportedly has a full calendar of waiting Russian celebrities, at the equivalent of $275 a session.

HEALING ENERGY—THE COMMONALITY

Those who practice arts of healing through touch—or the laying on of hands—have been called by a variety of names: shamans, witch doctors, mesmerists, faith healers, magnetic healers, energy healers, spiritual healers, and psychic healers. The modus operandi of history's healers differs widely; however, there is a single principle common to all the described modalities and their practitioners: the directed use of energy.

The foregoing observation led me to investigate the literature of energy healing. The present literature of energy healing consists of periodicals, books, sacred writings, brochures, technical and research reports, proceedings of meetings and symposia, dissertations and theses, unpublished works, reviews, audiovisual media, and electronic media.

These latter works largely describe paranormal phenomena, generally grounded in specific systems of belief, whose pre-and post-treatment results are not, or have not been, subjected to independent verification, and do not meet the level of proof currently required by Western scientific methods.

However, at the logical crossroads of twentieth-century *scientism* and five thousand years of personal testimony, rumor, legend, sacred writings, and recorded history, it is perhaps well to adopt an ancient philosophy— the philosophy of *probabilism:* certainty is impossible and that probability suffices to govern faith and practice (Faith and practice – Wilson Frank)

THE SPIRITUAL TRADITION

Through religious practices, (e.g., meditation and prayer), adepts of many religions claim to reach states of expanded consciousness, which open their latent higher – sense - perception abilities. These religious adherents speak of experiencing (or seeing) light around people's heads.

Ancient Indian spiritual tradition, over five thousand years old, describes a universal energy called *prana*. This universal energy is seen as the source of all life. Prana, the breath of life, moves through all forms to give them life. Yogis practice, manipulating this energy (through breathing techniques, meditation, and physical exercise) to attain altered states of consciousness, and longevity far beyond the normal life span.

In the third millennium B.C., the Chinese described the existence of a vital energy that they called Chi; they claimed that all matter, animate and inanimate, is composed of and permeated by this universal energy. This energy contains two polar forces, the *yin* and the *yang*. If the two polar forces are balanced, the subject organism exhibits physical health. In contrast, if yin and yang are unbalanced, a disease state results. Organic hyperactivity is said to be caused by excessive yang, while predominant yin makes for insufficient organic function. To summarize, imbalance of yin or yang is said to result in physical illness. Acupuncture, the ancient art of healing, by the insertion of needles, at specific bodily energy centers (acupuncture points), focuses on balancing the yin and the yang.

The Kabbalah, the Jewish mystical teaching, which originated around

538 B.C., refers to life-energy as the astral light. Christian paintings and sculpture show Jesus and other spiritual figures with a halo adorning their heads. Also, in the Old Testament, there are numerous references to light surrounding people and lights spontaneously appearing. In addition, sculpture and paintings of Buddha show a halo surrounding his head. Many gods of India are depicted, in both paintings and sculpture, with rays of energy or light emanating from their fingers.

THE SCIENTIFIC HISTORY OF SUBTLE ENERGY

<u>Early writings</u>.

The history of science also reflects a fascination with subtle energy. In 500 B.C., the Pythagoreans perceived an energy, which permeated all of nature: They claimed that its light could produce a variety of effects in the human body, including the healing of illness.

Liebault, writing in the early twelfth century, postulated that humans possess an energy that can react with, or promote interaction between, individuals—either at a distance or close by. He reported that, through this interaction, one person might have a healthful or unhealthful effect on another person, simply by being in his (or her) presence. In the middle ages, Paracelsus called this energy, illiaster. He defined illiaster as composed of vital force and a vital matter.

In the 1800s, the mathematician, Helmont, theoretically explained a universal fluid that pervades all nature—not a corporeal, or a condensable matter—but a therapeutic, vital spirit that penetrates all bodies. Further, the mathematician, Leibnitz, wrote that the essential elements of the universe are centers of force containing their own wellsprings of motion.

Mesmer, the father of modern hypnotism, observed that a field, similar to an electromagnetic field, exists around the human body, which he believed behaved as a fluid. He further believed that, through the vehicle of the field, human beings could also exert influence on each other at a distance.

Nineteenth-century observations.

In the mid-1800's, Count Wilhelm Von Reichenbach spent 30 years experimenting with an energy field, which he called the Odic force. He stated that this field had many properties that were similar to the electromagnetic field that James Clerk Maxwell had earlier observed. He also found many properties that were unique to the odic force. He determined that, with the odic force, like poles attract, i.e., like attract like. Subjectively, the poles of the odic force field exhibited the properties of being hot, red, and unpleasant—or cold, blue, and pleasant—to sensitive individuals. In addition, Von Reichenbach determined that opposite poles *do not* attract, as in electromagnetism. He also found that the odic field could be conducted through a wire; that the velocity of conduction was very slow, 13 feet per second (4 meters/second); and that the conduction velocity seemed to depend on the mass density of the material, rather than the electrical conductivity of the material. Von Reichenbach found that part of the odic field could be focused like a light through a lens, while another part of the odic field would flow around the lens, like a candle flame flows around something placed in its path of travel. He also found that air currents could also move this latter portion of the odic field, suggesting, perhaps, a gaseous composition.

Von Reichenbach's experiments indicate that the odic or auric field is energetic, like a light wave, and also particulate, like a fluid. His experiments also indicate that the *right side* of the body is a *positive* pole, and the *left* is *negative*. This is a concept that agrees with the ancient Chinese *yin* and *yang* principles.

Twentieth-century observations.

In the 1900s, interest in the Human Energy Field (HEF) was mounting in the medical community. In 1911, William Kilner, a medical doctor, practicing at St. Thomas' Hospital in London, reported on his studies of HEF—performed by looking through colored glass screens, stained with dicyanin dye. He claims to have seen a glowing mist around the subject's body in three zones: (a) a quarter-inch (0.6 cm) thick dark layer, closest to the skin; surrounded by, (b) a more vaporous layer, one-inch (2.5 cm) wide, streaming perpendicularly from the body; and (c) further out, a delicate exterior luminosity—with indefinite contours, about 6 inches (15 cm) wide.

Kilner observed that the appearance of the aura (as he called it) differs considerably from subject to subject, depending not only on age and sex; but also on their mental, physical, and emotional states. Based upon observations that certain diseases appeared as patches or irregularities in the aura, Kilner developed a system of medical diagnosis based upon observed patterns of auric irregularity. Using this latter system, Kilner successfully diagnosed various diseases: liver infection (hepatitis), tumors, appendicitis, epilepsy, and psychological disturbances, e.g., hysteria. His work is considered so impressive that, to this day, it remains the subject of European research.

In the mid-1900s, Drs. George De La Warr and Ruth Drown built new instruments to detect radiation from living tissues. They developed Radionics, a system of detection, diagnosis, and healing at a distance, using the human biological energy-field. The latter researchers took photographs, using the client's hair as an antenna: the resulting photographs showed internal diseases within living tissue, such as tumors and cysts within the liver, tuberculosis of the lungs, and cancer within the brain. Study of Radionics continues today in England.

In the early 1900's, Wilhelm Reich, a psychiatrist and colleague of Sigmund Freud, became an avid student of the universal field, which he named *orgone*. Reich studied the relationship between the disturbances of the *orgone* flow in the human body, and physical and psychological disease. He developed a psychotherapeutic modality, in which he used traditional methods of psychoanalysis, combined with methods of releasing orgone energy blockages. By the release of the orgone energy blocks, Reich could clear negative mental and emotional states. He subsequently constructed an accumulator, to concentrate the orgone energy; with the accumulator, Reich charged a vacuum discharge tube: the tube then conducted a current of electricity, at a potential lower than its normal discharge potential. Reich further claimed to increase the nuclear decay rate of a radioisotope, by placing the radioisotope in the orgone accumulator. Through the period of the 1930s through the 1950s, he experimented with orgone *energy*, using the latest electronic and medical instrumentation of the time: Reich sought to observe the orgone energy, which pulsates around all animate and inanimate objects.

More recently, the French microbiologist, Gustave Naessens, was concerned with hematological investigations: Naessens observed tiny particles in the blood, too small to identify with conventional microscopic equipment. He consequently developed a microscope, which he called the somatascope, to study these latter, dancing particles of light (the somatascope has a magnification of 30,000 diameters, and a resolution of 150 angstroms). In the somatid theory, Naessens states that cell division cannot take place without the presence of a minute life force, or energy particle, which he calls a somatid. Naessens postulates that the somatid is the original spark of life, the pinpoint where energy condenses into matter.

Drs. John and Eva Pierrakas have developed a system to diagnose and treat clients with psychological disorders, based upon visual and pendulum-based observations of the HEF. It was through information derived from these HEF observations, combined with psychotherapeutic methods, that the practice of *Bioenergetics* was developed: The Pierrakas' observations indicate that light emissions from the human body are closely related to health.

In work released in 1978, Drs. Pierrakas, Dr. Richard Dobrin, and Barbara Brennan measured the amplitude of a wavelength of light (approximately 350 nm), in a darkroom—before, during, and after people entered the room. The researchers observed a slight increase in the amplitude of (350 nm) light after a subject occupied the darkroom. However, when the subject in the room was feeling exhausted (or full of despair), the light value actually fell. With a *colorizer,* the researchers were able to show part of the auric field (the HEF), on a monochromatic monitor.

Another interesting study in *light emission* is the work of Hiroshi Motoyama. With a movie camera in a darkroom, Motoyama has measured low light levels coming from people who have practiced yoga for many years. Also, he studied the relative strengths of the energy meridians of healers and their respective clients—before and after treatment: Most of the time, the healers' energy level dipped—and then rose again. He also observed that the energy of the healer's heart chakra increased after treating a client.

Dr. Valerie Hunt and colleagues, at the University of California at Los Angeles (UCLA), have studied the correlation between changes in the very weak, natural electrical activity of the body's living tissues and a healer's perception of the body's energy field. Hunt placed electrodes on the skin to record the low voltage (mV) signals obtained from the human body during Rolfing sessions. These signals were fed into a video display, which produced waveforms of different colors on the screen. The Reverend Rosalyn Bruyere of the Healing Light Center (Glendale, California) was asked to observe the bodily *auras* and to record her observations of both the Rolfer and the client. Her observations were recorded on the same tape as the electronic data. Bruyere described the color, size, and energetic movements of the *chakras* (auric clouds, or HEF). Bruyere's perceptions were then matched against the electronic signals: both data were found to consistently agree. For example, when Bruyere reported seeing a blue aura emanating from the subject's body (as it was being massaged), the electrode connected to that area relayed a signal that produced a blue waveform on the display.

These foregoing observations seemed to indicate that healers could, in fact, pinpoint and identify the body's various energy emanations. Hunt also stated that chakras frequently carried the colors stated in the metaphysical literature, i.e., kundalini—red, *hypogastrium*—orange, spleen—yellow, heart—green, throat—blue, third eye—violet, and crown—white. Activity in certain chakras seemed to trigger increased activity in associated chakras. The heart chakra proved consistently to be the most active. Subjects had many emotional experiences; they also reported experiencing various sensory images and memory recalls, associated with those bodily areas Rolfed. These findings, in turn, gave credence to the hypothesis that memory of experiences is stored in bodily tissue.

According to Dr. Hunt, the workings of the human body can be viewed on a quantum-mechanical level: the atomic and, therefore, molecular and cellular behavior of the functioning body cuts across all tissues and systems. She suggests that a holographic view of the HEF would be highly informative. Holography may provide a biophysical technique for ultimately unifying the cosmological and mechanistic views of human physiology.

Dr. Robert Becker, a former professor of orthopedic surgery, at the State University of New York (SUNY) Health Science Center (Syracuse), mapped a complex *electrical field* of the human body; the field appears as a conformal projection of the body and the central nervous system. He named this field, the Direct Current Control System. Becker measured the amplitude and plotted the flow patterns of direct current (DC), which move over and through the body. Becker found that this DC field changes shape and strength with physiological and psychological changes. (Becker, 1985)

At Lanzhou University in China, Dr. Zheng Ronliang conducted scientific research on *Chigong*: He measured the *chi* radiated from the human body, by using a biological detector, made from a leaf vein connected to a quantum photoelectric device. He studied the *chi* emissions of a *Chigong master*, and compared the master's emissions with the energy field emanations of a *clairvoyant*: Ronliang found that the energy pulses emanating from the hands of the Chigong master are very different in nature from those of the clairvoyants. Studies conducted at Shanghai Atomic Nuclear Institute of Academia, Sinica, showed that some *vital force* emanations from Chigong masters seem to have a very low frequency, fluctuating carrier wave. *Chi* was detected as a micro-particle flow, with a particle size of 60 m in diameter, and a velocity of 20-50 cm/sec.

Extensive studies on the biophysical nature of consciousness have been conducted in Yugoslavia by Drs. Dejan Rakovic and Gordana Vitaliano. They assessed the possibility of HEF being associated with a low dielectric, ionic structure with an embedded, ultra-low-frequency electromagnetic field. They also described the development of a new consciousness-exhibiting, brain-like bio computer which would have a similar, ionic neural network.

Scientists from the Bio information Institute of A. S. Popov All-Union Scientific and Technical Society of Radio Technology and Electrical Communications started an intensive program on extra-sensory perception, in 1965. They used the methods of modern physicists in their experiments on *telepathy*. The scientists announced the discovery that living organisms emit vibrations at a frequency of 300 to 2,000 nm; they called this energy the biofield, or bioplasma. They showed that the biofield was stronger when people were more successful at transferring their bioenergy. The Medical Sciences Academy in Moscow confirmed these findings; moreover, these data are supported by research in Germany, Poland, the Netherlands, and Great Britain.

The existence of the *human energy field* (HEF) has been proved through studies conducted through Kirilian photography, somatid microscopy, light emission studies, electromagnetic field observations, and biophysics. Studies to explore (and explain) the HEF, continue unabated. Larry Dosey, M.D.—former chief of staff at Humana Hospital (Dallas,

Texas) and the author of many books on healing—predicts that what scientists and medical doctors know now about energy healing "is just a preview of coming attractions." When better-designed scientific research confirms existing studies on energy healing, Dossey says: "we'll look back and wonder what took us so long." Across the sciences, from physics to medicine and biology, researchers are on the verge of major paradigm shifts in understanding how the universe operates. We used to rely on a mechanistic, Newtonian model of the universe. We were led to believe that the earth operates like a grand machine, and that we could learn about it by breaking it down into its component parts, learning about each part in isolation. Now, we realize how little such reductionism has taught us about the integrated behavior of the earth's planetary systems—let alone interplanetary and intergalactic systems. For example, we now know that time and space is not isolated dimensions; rather, time and space are aspects of a continuum known as space-time.

THE FUTURE OF HEALING ENERGY RESEARCH.

In the twentieth-century, we have begun to explore a *universal model*, based upon Einsteinian relativity: a complex and interconnected universe of particle and energy fields, in which matter and energy are interconvertible. We are finally coming to accept the *probability* that universal systems are interactive, and that we, human beings, are an integral part of these systems—and of the *whole*.

Recently, in a lecture for the International Society for the Study of Subtle Energies and Energy Medicine, Dr. Larry Dossey recounted an old story that is a metaphor for man's progress toward understanding universal laws:

"There was once an argument among the gods over where to hide the secret of life so that men and women would not find it. One god said: Bury it under a mountain; they will never look there. No, the others said, one day they will find ways to dig up mountains and will uncover it. Another said: Sink it in the depths of the ocean; it will be safe there. No the others objected, humans will one day find a way to plumb the ocean's depths and find it easily. Finally another god said: Put it inside them; men and women will never think of looking for it there. All the gods agreed, and so that is how the secret of life came to be hidden within us."

I believe that we are now approaching the time when we will finally unlock our inner wisdom, learn to look inside of ourselves for the secret of life, and therefore honor our interconnectedness to everything in the universe. We will then understand our influence on all persons and things around us. We will become aware that our emotions and thoughts play a *major role* in our physical health. *Energy healing* will then cease to be considered *paranormal;* rather, we will come to *re-discover* an ancient wisdom: the truly *effective* way to treat physical illness is through comprehension of the human being as a whole.

UNIVERSAL ENERGY

When Albert Einstein wrote the equation, "$E = mc^2$," he threw science into a tailspin. He postulated that there was no difference between matter and energy. Matter, as well as energy, is composed of various particles. If the particles stick together, the result is matter; if they do not, the result is energy. One is always a form of the other.

We, human beings, are matter which result from the combination of complex fields of life-energy that are coextensive with the universe. Human beings are maintained by an ocean of nutritious energy, comparable to the amniotic liquid in which a fetus floats.

The old scientific idea that the world is made up of purely solid material has disappeared; that idea has been replaced by a new concept of the universe filled with, up till now, unimaginable energy. As part of that universe, we no longer conceive of our world, and therefore ourselves, our physical bodies, as purely solid matter.

We are daily breaking the boundaries of the spaces surrounding and within our planet. Increasingly advanced technology is employed to research the sub-microscopic, internal spaces of physical matter. We are moving to a multidimensional appreciation of the space-time continuum and matter-energy interactions heretofore unknown.

Einstein's vision of a complex universe with time and energy fields extending through space (i.e., the existence of a life energy flowing through and around all of us) is a hypothesis that cannot be completely observed by present-day scientific instruments. Its constituents are not solely formed from alpha, beta or gamma radiation, from electromagnetic radiation (radio waves) or from electrostatic, ultrasonic, gravitational or magnetic energy: It is a form of energetic behavior that is largely undiscovered by science and which exceeds the limitations of all known sensor technology.

We are so conditioned to consider only what we can see, touch, or measure that we hardly give any thought to this latter universe of energy, and what *life energy* means within its context. However, today's researchers are spending a great deal of time studying the *human energy field* and how it affects our physical body.

HUMAN ENERGY

The existence of a human energy field cannot be denied. Its influence on the physical body has been measured by devices like the electroencephalograph (EEG), the electrocardiograph (ECG/EKG), and the SQUID (a highly sensitive magnetometer).

Researchers like Robert O. Becker, M.D. (a professor of orthopedic surgery, formerly at the State University of New York Health Science Center in Syracuse and the author of *Body Electric: Electromagnetism and the Foundation of life*), measured patterns of direct current electricity that flow over and through the body. Dr. Becker showed that the pattern, shapes and strengths of the body's complex electrical field change with physiological and psychological changes. He conducted a series of studies documenting the presence of electromagnetic energy in the body. He found that the meridians are actually electrical conductors that carry messages of injury and pain to the brain. The brain responds by sending back to the injured area a current, which is really a message about how to stimulate healing. This *subtle energy* has not, as yet, been scientifically proved; however, emerging research, similar to Dr. Becker's, continues to unfold its reality.

Many of us (indeed, most of us) cannot *visualize* the human energy field. I am sure; however, many of us have *felt* its presence, although we may have been unable to fully describe it. Do you remember the last time that you were in someone's presence and, before any words had been said, you *knew* something was wrong? At that moment, you were experiencing that person's energy field. How many times have you been feeling depressed and, after being in the presence of someone who is very happy and energetic, you discover that you are feeling substantially elevated in mood? Is the happiness "contagious"? No, it is the interpersonal interaction of human energy fields produces the effect.

"ALL HUMAN BEINGS HAVE THE ABILITY TO BECOME HEALERS"

The reality of this latter interpersonal exchange of energy is the foundation for my personal theory that all human beings have the ability to become healers. It is not a gift bestowed upon a chosen few; rather, it is each human being's birthright to have his or her emotional and physical being made healthy. Co-equally, it is each human being's birth responsibility to extend to those around us our healing touch.

We, all of us, are healers: you probably have healed yourself and others many times, not even knowing it. When you hurt yourself, what is the first thing you do? You guard the site of injury with your hand, holding it. It is a natural instinct; however, if you pay attention the next time an injury occurs, you will notice that the hand that is holding the injured part will get hot. It is the healing energy flowing from your hand to the injured area.

When someone you love is going thorough emotional pain, what do you do? You hold your loved one. When you are emotionally depressed, don't you feel better after a hug? These latter examples show the simplicity of energetic human healing: All that you require is a loving empathy toward those experiencing pain.

Do not allow the lack of knowledge stop you. However, the more educated you become in the manipulation of subtle energies and more knowledgeable about the physical body (vs. the energy of the human body) the greater is the probability that you will enjoy successfully healing others. With this Knowledge it will be easier to accomplish your work.

It is time for each of us to stop thinking about ourselves as purely physical beings, having occasional spiritual experiences; we must come to focus upon our *true* nature: a spiritual being having a physical experience.

It is as spiritual beings that we are; we carry within us our soul mission, a personal mission to be accomplished within this lifetime. I was fortunate enough to discover my soul mission: It is to be not only a healer, but to awaken others to the tremendous potential hidden within each of us —to heal others and ourselves.

Discovery of my soul mission was the motivation for me to write this book. I hope that when you finish reading this book, you will reach out to someone near you and share with that person your individual gift of healing, in the firm belief that you can make a difference with your loving empathy, your human compassion.

UNDERSTANDING THE HUMAN ENERGY FIELD

The literature concerning *hands-on* healing is rather extensive. There are so many healing methods and techniques with which to become acquainted, that the novice healer may soon become confused and, thus, quickly discouraged.

The most important point to remember, however, is *how* the subtle energies influence the physical body. No matter what method the prospective healer may choose to work with, he (or she) will be working with energy.

As mentioned before, each of us has the power to heal. Each of us can create miracles in our lives and in the lives of our loved ones, simply by opening our hearts to love, compassion, and the desire to heal.

If it be the reader's intention to become a professional healer, I would highly recommend that the reader first become familiar with the spectrum of healing techniques available. Secondly, let him (or her) choose a healing technique that has especial personal resonance. And, thirdly, the prospective healer should enroll in classes with an experienced healer and teacher.

This book will provide an introduction to different healing techniques, and its bibliography is offered as a resource for those just embarked on a mission of healing. Beware, however, that becoming a professional healer requires the exercise of personal responsibility; and *that* responsibility includes education.

In this chapter I will concentrate on the study of the human energy field, the subtle body, the chakras, and the light body: a basic understanding of the latter four topics is fundamental knowledge; knowledge which is prerequisite for students of energy healing.

Universal Energy

The assumption of a universal life-energy is currently linked to field theory; life-energy is perceived as displaying the characteristics of a force field.

In physical science, a field is generally defined as a continuous quality or condition through space. For example, it is a fact that gravity, as a field, exists everywhere in space: however, it is observed to be more intense in the area around a planet or other celestial body. Considering that life is the dynamics of the universe, one may well assume that vital energy also exists as a force field; i.e., that it penetrates space, becoming more concentrated within and around living organisms. Thus, in the same way that all physical objects in the universe are subject to the force of gravity, we may postulate that all living things, without exception, exist in a universal life-energy field.

Indeed, communication (energetic interaction) with all living *bodies* around us is an inherent characteristic of the human condition, as Caroline Myss (1996, p. 33, 34) explains in her book, Anatomy of the Spirit: "Your physical body is surrounded by an energy field that extends as far out as your outstretched arms and the full length of your body. It is both an information center and a highly sensitive perceptual system, which is a kind of conscious electricity that transmits and receives messages to and from other people's bodies."

Further, we carry the emotional energy from all of our life experiences in our subtle (energy) body, including past and present relationships (both personal and professional), as well as traumatic experiences.

The Subtle Body

The formative-field body or what Theosophists call the subtle body is the first of the levels of being beyond the physical body. This subtle body is the subtle life-force body, which sustains the life of the physical body and serves as the mold for physical, metabolic functions.

The subtle body is the absorber of the fluid of life (vital fluid) called prana. The subtle body is rarely separated from the physical body during earthly life; however, separation does occur when certain drugs, e.g., anesthetics, are administered. The subtle body is the true source of all physical vitality. The subtle body is also responsible for sensations, general body consciousness, and a form of awareness higher than simple, organic, physical cognizance.

The physical and the subtle bodies are correctly grouped together: they both function on the physical plane; they are inextricably interlinked, the energy body surrounding the physical body; both are discarded by the human spirit at death; and, as one disintegrate, so disintegrates the other.

Barbara Brennan (1993), reports that the subtle body is comprised of seven layers. The first three layers of the subtle body are associated with indeed, mediate—those energy flows related to the physical world.

First layer - the etheric body. The first layer is the closest layer of the subtle body to the physical body and forms the energy matrix that gives the physical body structure. It is through this level that one feels all physical pain. Pain, in physical body parts, shows as a dysfunction within the first layer of one's auric field (subtle body).

Second layer - the emotional body. The second layer is associated with feelings and emotions. Its color varies according to one's emotional state.

Third layer - the mental body. The third layer is associated with thoughts and mental processes.

The succeeding four layers of the subtle body are associated with the spiritual world:

The fourth layer - the astral level. The fourth layer of the subtle body has been described to be intimately associated with relationships and human interactions.

The fifth layer - the etheric template. The fifth layer is the blueprint or perfect form for the etheric body or first layer. The fifth layer holds the first layer in place.

The sixth layer - the celestial body. The sixth layer is associated with spiritual bliss; it contains the ecstasy of our spirituality. It is through the celestial body that we experience spirituality.

The seventh layer - the universal mind field. The seventh layer contains our Higher Truth: the purpose of our soul. The seventh layer embodies our understanding of God.

Respecting and learning to experience our subtle bodies helps us to rekindle our true nature, our universal interconnectedness. In this way, we can learn to sense the world with the wholeness of our being. Instead of relying solely upon our physical senses (which we have come to accept as the only valid sensors of the physical world), we can come to perceive the play of events surrounding us in the very depths of who and what we are. Rather than succumbing to the narrow channels through which sensory information enters the physical body, filtered by our partiality and inclination, we can become conscious of the greater reality of our Source, to which we are destined to return.

THE CHAKRA SYSTEM

Understanding that one's body does not end at outer skin level (the epidermis); i.e., remaining mindful of the surrounding, seven-layered subtle body, the reader is now prepared to address the third of four topics of fundamental knowledge, knowledge prerequisite for work in energy healing: the chakra system.

Brennan describes the subtle body as having a main power current running vertically, up and down the spine. She describes the chakras as energetic vortices, with the open ends traveling out through the layers of the subtle body and the narrow vortex tips emanating from the central, vertical channel. The crown and basal chakras open out top and bottom, respectively; the remaining five open out to the front of the body, with counterparts opening out to the back.

It was previously noted that the subtle body is comprised of seven layers: Brennan also reports that each chakra also possesses seven layers, one in each layer of the subtle body. The tip of the chakra, where it enters the central energy channel, is called the root. The root of the chakra acts as a valve, which controls the flow of energy from one level to another. The chakras themselves exchange energy with the Universal Energy Field, and act as arbiters of energy exchange between the different levels.

The Chakras

Eastern culture teaches us that a great deal of stress and anxiety can be reduced by an inner workout, which purpose is to harmonize and balance one's chakra system. To balance and harmonize one's chakra system, one must become aware of the existence of chakras and learn about each chakra's influence upon one's physical body.

Around the world, healers agree that all disease starts in one's subtle body, before manifesting or materializing in one's physical body. Viewing bodily health from this perspective, one soon realizes that one could treat diseases (eliminate or reduce the severity thereof) and/or mitigate disease symptoms, before their materialization in the physical body, by working with the chakras.

This foregoing concept, alone, is a great motivation for the reader to become knowledgeable about the chakras as part of one's being. In the paragraphs that follow, I summarize information, which has been gathered from the available literature and supplemented with personal experience in working with subtle energy centers. I also include information about the chakras personally acquired through channeling. The following writing could well be titled, "How the chakras are seen from spiritual realms."

Chakra is a Sanskrit word for wheel. Chakras are subtle energy centers located in one's subtle energy body. There are *seven major chakras*, and several minor ones. When these subtle energy centers are perceived, they look like wheels of spinning light. Barbara Brennan (1993, p. 26, 28) reports that according to her Higher Sense Perception. The chakras look much more like vortices, or funnels, of energy. They exist on each of the seven levels of the field, and chakras two through six appear on both the front and the back of the body. Each funnel has its wider opening on the outside of our body, about six inches in diameter, one inch from the body. The small tip is inside of the body near the spine.

Whereas the physical body represents our gross anatomy, the system of chakras represents our subtle anatomy. A chakra can be thought of as being an oscillator with a unique (natural) resonant frequency. An oscillator can be described as any object that moves in a regular periodic manner, such as a violin string or a pendulum. Two oscillators having the same natural frequency can develop sympathetic resonance, which means that the vibrations of one oscillator can reinforce those of the other.

When the seven energy centers (chakras) are in perfect resonance, subtle energy flows throughout the nervous system—facilitating a feeling of peace and well-being.

Each wheel of energy (chakra) spins with one of the seven colors of the rainbow. The chakras withdraw energy from universal life-energy, process it, and send it to the part of the body closest to it. If there is dysfunction in a chakra, the distribution of energy will be disturbed: The part of the body supplied by said chakra would become depleted of energy. If this latter dysfunction in distribution of energy persists, the affected part of the body will weaken and disease will eventually occur.

Within each one of the chakras is a seed of consciousness represented by the emotion that is held there. We hold our emotions in each one of the seven chakras.

From the above discussion, it becomes clear that knowledge of the chakras greatly aids in the practice of energy healing by facilitating the assessment of the underlying *cause* of the client's disease. Also, knowledge of the color resonating within each chakra, aids in the visualization process of energy healing.

The first chakra.

The first chakra is the *root chakra* or *basic chakra*. Its color is red; it governs the kidneys, the adrenals, and the spinal column. Its male location is at the bottom (root) of the spine, between the anal sphincter and the scrotum; analogously, in females, it is located between the anal sphincter and the vaginal orifice. The external vortical opening faces downwards, between one's legs. It is the chakra energy center closest to the earth; its basis is survival, rooting, support, and grounding.

Parts of the body influenced by the root chakra are the adrenals, immune system, kidneys, spinal column, colon, legs, and bones. Physical conditions related to the first chakra include chronic lower back problems, varicose veins, rectal tumors and cancer, immune disorders, kidney problems, and joint and bone problems in the lower extremities. Mental health disorders associated with the first chakra include: depression, obsessive-compulsive disorders, addictions, phobias, and anxiety.

It is through the root chakra that we feel grounded to the earth. It is also through this chakra that we feel fear. It controls the mechanism of fight or flight. The root chakra is also the chakra that governs material living; it is the subtle energy center that roots the divine consciousness in material life. Consequently, it is the basis for human existence in this physical world. When vital energy in the root chakra is blocked, we feel rootless in our spiritual and physical existence.

The energy from the root chakra is the energy we use to rouse ourselves from slumber in the morning, and to go about the business of our day. It represents the first step into the material world. Positive qualities of the first chakra include matters relating to the material world, stability, tranquility, health, courage, patience, the ability to defend oneself, and grounding. Correspondingly, negative qualities associated with the root chakra include insecurity, greed, fears of abandonment, anger, violence, and over-concern about one's physical survival.

Every human being has a joint physical and spiritual existence. Karmic development causes an oscillation between the spiritual and the physical dimensions; when the karmic process goes positively, one feels tranquil both dimensions.

The first chakra is the grounding point, the point of the soul's attachment to physical life. It is through the physical grounding of a mother's love, the bonding between mother and child during the nursing period, that a newborn child will gather the needed strength to function in the physical world.

Moreover, in facilitating the bonding between mother and child, the newborn's separation from the spiritual realm (from which it recently departed) is made easier. That is why the nursing period is so important for human beings. During the time of nursing, both the mother and the child will have stimulated, developed, and cleansed their first chakras. This early experience of physical grounding gives the newborn child a developmental head start, which cannot be otherwise obtained.

The second chakra.

The second chakra is the sexual chakra. Its color is orange; it governs attitudes toward relationships, sex, reproduction, and creativity. Located about one inch below the navel, the second chakra affects all the fluid systems in the body: the urinary system, the lymph, etc. Moreover, the second chakra affects ovaries in the female and testes in the male; it also governs the large intestine, lower vertebrae, pelvis, appendix, bladder, and hip area.

Physical problems related to this chakra are blood disorders, obstetrical and gynecological problems, sexual impotency, urinary disorders, prostate or ovarian cancer, difficulties associated with menopause, uterine tumors, and depression.

Balancing the second chakra releases sexual tension and unleashes creativity. Indeed, it is through this latter chakra that one develops sexuality and enhances personal creativity. If blocked, however, the ability to maintain life-balance is jeopardized.

The positive qualities associated with the sexual chakra include giving and receiving, emotions, pleasure, sexual passion and desire, change, movement, health, family, assimilation of new ideas, tolerance, endurance (especially financial staying power), the ability to take risks, personal empowerment, and freedom to make choices. Concomitant negative qualities include: overindulgence in food or sex, sexual difficulties, confusion, jealousy, desire to possess, fear of losing control or being controlled by others, tendency toward financial loss, and the inability to protect oneself.

Sexual purity will balance and enhance this chakra. Because there have always been social taboos concerning sex and, it has been said, that sex in itself is impure—further explanation on the topic of sexual purity is required: Sex is only impure, if it is practiced for solely egoistic reasons, and/or by hurting others.

When two people make love, the vortical lights from their individual, sexual chakras are mixed; these positively reinforcing light waves create figure-like displays, the beauty of which is governed by the intensity of love between the parties. During sexual embrace, two people who truly love one another create a surrounding aura that can be compared to a forest of fairytale trees, whose flowers and leaves create an arc above the lovers. The energetic vibrations of chakras thus merged are so powerful, that much *negative karma* can be burned away.

Simply stated, by selflessly loving another person (and demonstrating it through sexual behavior that pleases and satisfies one's partner), one can undergo profound personal and spiritual development. Sexual purity further implies that a bond of love exists between the two persons, that there is a willingness to give freely to one another, and that both prepared to abandon egoistic demands in favor of interpersonal giving.

The third chakra.

The third chakra is the *solar plexus chakra*. The color of the third chakra is yellow. The third chakra governs the pancreas, liver, spleen, stomach, gall bladder, and some aspects of the nervous system. Its location is the central cavity of the lungs. Its basis is personal power and metabolic energy. Its primal essence is that of the will. Its foundation is based on one's individual nature.

The physical organs influenced by the third chakra are the abdomen, stomach, upper intestines, liver, gallbladder, pancreas, adrenal glands, middle spine, muscles, and the nervous system. The solar plexus chakra is the energy field that resonates with our emotional responses. It anchors the life stream, which governs the circulation of blood throughout the body. It's also vitalizes the sympathetic branch of the autonomic nervous system (which controls involuntary muscle, viscera and glands, mobilizing the body for action).

Physical problems related to the third chakra include arthritis, gastric problems, ulcers, colon or intestinal problems, diabetes, indigestion, anorexia or bulimia, liver dysfunction and disease, and adrenal dysfunction.

The positive qualities of the solar plexus chakra include will, personal power, energy, mastery of desire, self-control, warmth, humor, laughter, awakening, balanced self-esteem, self-respect, self-control, care for oneself and others, personal honor, trust, the ability to handle a crisis, generosity, and positive ethical standards. Negative qualities corresponding to the third chakra include: lack of will power, coldness, absent of humor, lack of discipline, low self-esteem, inability to handle crisis, and lack of consideration for others.

In a normal human being, the third chakra is considered to be developed when it is capable of resonating emotions, which incorporate both feelings from the emotional body and concrete thoughts from the mental body. This latter chakra is the energy center for all personal feelings: feelings of personal power, feelings of vulnerability, and feelings of sensitivity. It is in this chakra that we carry anger, hostility, and rage. Moreover, the third chakra governs reactive energy to perceived threats: events that threaten our personal power, freedom of will, and the ability to achieve our personal ambitions. It is in the solar plexus chakra that we blunt our emotional sensitivity. The solar plexus chakra gives us more problems than any other chakra, because it is essentially the seed of emotional life. Quite characteristically, imbalanced emotions evidence themselves as digestive disorders.

When two people argue, the light in their respective, solar plexus chakras darkens. The light waves from the combatant chakras negatively reinforce one another. Disturbing figures of light can be perceived in the vicinity of the disputants, and it is common to see small blue-violet ogres above the people who are arguing. The darker the blue-violet light is, the greater the hatred is manifested between the two. When the merged light from the combatant chakras changes from indigo to black, a blockage may then occur in the solar plexus chakra (in one or both of them).

The foregoing analysis of negative reinforcement, regarding the chakras of arguing parties, does not mean that one should not attempt to resolve his (or her) problems with others. Rather, the key is how one approaches problem resolution. There is a difference between argument and confrontation.

To argue is to war with another: one attacks; the other feels treated, complains, and counter-attacks. Conversely, confrontation (a form of one-on-one psychological intervention) requires that each of the parties (a) explains his (or her) point of view concerning the matter disputed, (b) shares his (or her) feelings which have arisen from or contributed to the dispute, and (c) accomplishes the latter explaining and sharing without malice or further argument.

Constructive confrontations are presently utilized in-group psychotherapy to achieve behavioral breakthroughs not otherwise attainable. Confrontation is a healing tool for unblocking the solar plexus chakra. If you are engaged in interpersonal conflict, you cannot resolve the conflict by denial. However, if you agree to restrict yourself to the specific matter in dispute; and, if you stand peacefully prepared to resolve the conflict, then you will have expressed love, respect, and a desire for fair play. At this critical juncture, confrontation can be transformed into negotiated agreement; both parties are willing to resolve the conflict without further attacking one another. On the other hand, unresolved problems in our relationships with others manifest themselves as unrelieved muscle tensions, indigestion, nausea, and blockages in many different areas.

The fourth chakra.

The fourth chakra is the *heart chakra*. The color of the heart chakra is green. The heart chakra governs the activity of the heart; the circulatory system, including the blood within; and it has a very strong influence on the immune system. Its location is about 2-3 inches (5-7.5 cm) above the solar plexus. The fourth chakra extends through the organ of the heart from the central vertical channel; its vertical area is the general area between the pleural cavity and the pericardium.

Some of the organs associated with the fourth chakra are the heart, lungs, shoulder, arms, ribs, breast, diaphragm, thymus gland, and circulatory system (blood is a tissue). The fourth chakra also controls the vagus nerve, the largest nerve in the parasympathetic branch of the autonomic nervous system, a branch nervous system that acts in opposition to the sympathetic nervous system, e.g., inhibiting the heartbeat or constricting the pupil of the eye.

Physical illnesses that can be trigged by the fourth chakra are myocardial infarction (heart attack), cardiovascular disease, asthma, allergies, lung cancer, bronchial problems, shoulder and upper back problems, and breast cancer.

The bases of the fourth chakra are love, human associations, human relations, and compassion. Its primal essence is the act of interrelation, and all actions that fall within the scope of love. The fourth chakra is the chakra through which we fall in love.

With respect to the *subtle body*, we do not fall "upwards" in love; rather, we fall "downwards" in love. First, we fall in love *through* this subtle energy center; then, we naturally move that love down to the emotional center, the solar plexus chakra; and, ultimately, we feel the manifestation of love in the sexual chakra. It is through love, emotionality, and sexuality that we progressively move downwards to the grounding chakra, the first chakra, whereat we experience tranquility and the feeling of "settling down."

Positive qualities associated with the fourth chakra are unconditional love of self (and others), trust, understanding, forgiveness, acceptance, openness, peace, harmony, and contentment. Negative qualities associated with the fourth chakra are self-revulsion (and, correspondingly, loathing of others), self-doubt (and mistrust of others), lack of understanding, anger, grief, hopelessness, lack of compassion, dysfunctional relationships with family (and others), lovelessness, and lack of friendships.

The heart chakra deals with love and harmony. It is the most important chakra of the seven chakras: it contains the seed for our ability to experience the Divine—pure love for everyone and everything. *Pure love* is love that is absent egoism, calculation, artifice, or demand for reciprocity.

When observing two people who love each other purely, they are seen together surrounded by figures of light and beauty quite beyond description—like a rose-pink rainbow, shining in all directions. Indeed, flowers in the most beautiful and harmonious rose-pink colors can be seen above them.

All intellectual knowledge is utterly subordinate to our ability to experience love. Learning to love is what God demands of us mortal beings; and it is our only real demand for spiritual development. God is pure love; and, our foremost duty during this mortal stay, our return journey to Him, is to learn to feel this *pure love* for others.

The fifth chakra.

The fifth chakra is the throat chakra. The throat chakra's color is blue; it governs the thyroid gland, the vocal cords and the trachea. Its location is about the midway point between the skull and the lower neck cavity. It is about one inch inward from the throat. It is in linear vertical alignment with the spinal cord. Some of the organs associated with the fifth chakra include the afore-mentioned thyroid gland, the throat, the trachea, neck (cervical) vertebrae, the mouth, gums, teeth, and esophagus. Some of the illnesses related to the fifth chakra are chronic sore throats, mouth ulcers, gum (periodontal) difficulties, joint problems, laryngitis, swollen glands, thyroid problems, throat cancer, chronic dental problems, and scoliosis.

The bases of the throat chakra are communication, creativity, and judgment. Inner work on the throat chakra will surface frustrating issues in communication that require resolution. With further effort, use of language and other forms of communication will become more an expression of one's innate spiritual maturity; one's voice becomes clear and deepens. Through the fifth chakra we question the wisdom of self-expression; we come to be more concerned with the judgment of others.

Positive qualities associated with the throat chakra include good communication skills, appropriate personal expression, using personal power to create, positive faith and knowledge, truth, wisdom, loyalty, good writing and artistic skills, the ability to make choices, willpower, reliability, and kindness.

Corresponding negative qualities of the fifth chakra can be inadequate (or absent) communication skills, lying, dishonesty, hiding the truth from self (and others), feeling out of control, lack of willpower, fears, ignorance, using one's knowledge unwisely, inability to make decisions, and lack of faith.

The fifth chakra radiates a clear blue color: not light blue, but a clear blue color, like the sky on a clear summer day. When our throat chakra is balanced, we feel an inner, completely unshakeable peace; we feel strong, no matter the circumstances. Strength arising from the fifth chakra is not concerned with physical might, per se; rather, it is an expression of inner strength, a strength that springs from trusting in oneself, and trusting in one's higher (divine) self.

When two people merge the energies from their respective throat chakras, they do so by speaking to each other actively and intensely. If one or both speakers attempt(s) to dominate the discussion, the joint blue color turns dark: Figures of light in the form of weapons may appear above the two. Conversely, if two people merge energies from their respective throat chakras, without the desire for domination, the most beautiful blue color subsequently appears. Within this color, which symbolizes strength and solidarity, humorous figures (like laughing fairies) can be seen—for when there are no dark overtones of a struggle for power between speakers, humor naturally springs forth. Therefore, a sense of humor is an excellent quality to cultivate; moreover, a good joke (should the conversation turn unpleasant) is an exercise in wisdom and maturity, because humor is universally disarming.

The sixth chakra.

The sixth chakra is the *brow chakra* or the *third eye chakra*. The color of the sixth chakra is indigo (a deep violet-blue). The sixth chakra governs the brain, the pineal and pituitary glands, and the central nervous system. The sixth chakra is located in the center of the forehead between the eyes, often referred to as the *third eye* or *ajna center*.

Described in part, above, the sixth chakra vitalizes the cerebellum (lower brain) and central nervous system (which consists of nerve fibers within the brain stem and spinal cord) and further governs the ears (sense of hearing) and nose (sense of smell). Positive qualities of the third eye chakra include intellectual and emotional abilities, intuition, imagination, clairvoyance, concentration, wisdom, devotion, insight, and peace of mind. Concomitant negative qualities include an unwillingness to look at oneself, tension, frightening dreams, detachment from the world, fear of sounds, fear of external counseling, fears relating to spiritual issues, feelings of inadequacy, lack of concentration, loss of identity, loss of connection with life and people around us, mental confusion, and alienation.

Illnesses associated with the sixth chakra include brain tumors, strokes, neurological problems, problems with one's eyesight, hearing problems, learning disabilities, agoraphobia (a morbid fear of crossing—or of being— in open or public places), seizures, headaches, and migraines.

Working with the third eye chakra involves becoming conscious of what we believe in and the world around us; moreover, it involves working-through (self-examination and conquest) thoughts that involve self-pity, anger, fears, or blame. This chakra involves our mental faculties and reasoning abilities. It resonates energy to our minds, so that we may begin to seriously question our spiritual nature. It forces us to compare and contrast our inner vision of self with our outward manifestation of self. Our positive, creative visualizations are outwardly projected to the world through the third eye chakra. Concentration and inner focus also occur in this chakra: through the inner vision of the brow chakra, we can direct the outward manifestation of our desired vision in life. Further, idealism and imagination are centered in this chakra: if one can dream of it, one can accomplish it. When developed, the sixth chakra focuses wisdom, insight, and spiritual purpose (all received through the crown chakra), which then can be used to control one's personality. It is the center for clairvoyance, visions, and transcendence of time and space in thinking. Enhancing the third eye chakra involves becoming conscious of what we believe in, and the world around us, as well as cleansing oneself from thoughts that involve self-pity, anger, fear, or blame.

Although the physical color for the sixth chakra is indigo, this chakra radiates a clear *green* light. Those who have begun to develop skills in clairvoyance have a shining green ball located in the area of the third eye chakra. This ball protects, and draws energy into the brain. Also, when two people blend the energies from their respective third-eye chakras, their clairvoyance increases. Restated, if both clairvoyants have relatively clean and pure third-eye energy centers, their understanding of unknowns will be increased considerably; in addition, figures of light appear around them which are also beautiful, shining, and green. When two people with *very clear* third-eye centers meld, their conjoined energies may be perceived as a ring, showing the entire story of creation; and within the unfolded panorama of creation, within the entire dimension of time, a deep understanding of what has transpired in each of their lives becomes revealed. However, if one (or both) has an unclean third-eye chakra, the would-be clairvoyants exhibit third eye chakras that have turned dark green and have become muddied. Misconceptions of time and space occur.

From the spiritual perspective, much can be learned about one's personality, especially with respect to third-eye problems. For example, relationships tend to intensify anomalies of the third-eye chakra. If two persons are married, and the one has a very unclean third-eye chakra, the other must be careful not to become affected by the totality of maladies that arise therefrom. Problems with the third-eye chakra are very often the reason for divorce, because problems with the brow chakra are intuitively felt by the party with the cleanest chakra. This latter revelation is not made to encourage parties to divorce; however, if one's chakras are relatively clean and he (or she) is steadily progressing toward spiritual enlightenment, he (or she) needs to become aware of how to protect himself (or herself) against negative influences. If you are especially concerned about avoiding blockage of the third-eye chakra, you should simply pray to God for a semi-permanent ring of protection on this area.

The seventh chakra.

The seventh chakra is the *crown chakra*. The crown chakra's color is violet. The seventh chakra is located at the pivotal axis point of the skull, at the very top. The organs governed by the seventh chakra are the skin, the skeletal and muscular systems, and the cerebral cortex. The crown chakra vitalizes the cerebrum (or upper brain) and anchors the consciousness stream from the causal body (or soul), enabling a person to have self-awareness.

Physical problems related does the seventh chakra include energy disorders, mental disorders, chronic exhaustion, and hypersensitivity to light and sound. Meditation and positive spirituality helps keep this chakra clear to receive energy without interference. The positive qualities of a developed seventh chakra are unification with the higher self, a fully integrated human personality, spiritual will, inspiration, divine wisdom, comprehensive understanding, insightfulness, and spiritual purpose. Correspondingly, the negative qualities related to the crown chakra include fears related to spiritual issues, loss of personal identity, and loss of connectedness to life and to those around us, mental confusion, and alienation.

The bases of the crown chakra are knowledge, information, understanding, and refined thoughts. The seventh chakra is the connection to one's spirituality. It is also the entry point for the life force that pours energy into the entire chakra system. The seventh chakra is the energy center most associated with divine issues and their accomplishment. It is through the seventh chakra that we actively attempt to integrate ourselves with whatever our understanding of God is, and align ourselves with limitless consciousness: It is the attempt to reconcile our interior and exterior consciousness into a harmonious whole. The crown chakra is symbolized by the thousand-fold lotus, because this chakra deals with issues beyond translation and beyond our linear understanding of the space-time continuum: It deals with aspects truly beyond human comprehension. It is through this energy center that the body and the spirit are fused. Within the crown chakra, there exist representative counterparts of the other six, major chakras. When the crown chakra is balanced, profound relaxation occurs.

The seventh chakra is the most penetrable chakra to light. The crown chakra represents wisdom, deep and all-embracing wisdom. When the seventh chakra is clean, one experiences superior knowledge and understanding of everything. Nothing is obscure concerning life.

When two people mix energies from their crown chakras, as they speak to one another, the throat chakra is often involved because the act of speaking involves the throat chakra. Consequently, the lights from the crown chakra and the throat chakra are often admixed. If the crown chakras of the speakers are clean, it is relatively unimportant if they have a verbal dialogue, because the chakra's light will be telepathically communicated. A silent transference of wisdom from one to the other will take place, and no words will be necessary. Many will probably recognize the latter phenomenon from personal experience, where complete understanding of another occurs without the need for words to be spoken. Wisdom can also be transferred from one to another through the eyes.

When a person has a very clean crown chakra, a soft golden light envelops one's personal aura, which has a most beautiful and excellent influence on others. When two people with blocked crown chakras are speaking to one another, a very unpleasant color is observed (a muddy, dark curry color appears) which sensitive observers easily perceive. A tingling sensation is felt in the crowns of the speakers; their heads feel uncomfortable. When two people whose crown chakras are unclean unite, misconceptions occur that suggest mortal limitations, limitations in time and space; indeed, the misconception that one can only live once.

The eighth Chakra

The eighth chakra that was not even mentioned in many books about healing and the chakra system has become very popular lately. A simple search in the internet will offer you thousands of pages talking about the eighth chakra, with various interpretations of its color, location and purpose. As an Integrated Energy Therapy® practitioner, I prefer to stay with this healing system's understanding of the eighth chakra. Under this conception the eighth chakra is located about four feet above our head and its shape is oval, surrounding our entire body. In other words, considering that the fourth layer of our aura, the spiritual layer, is also four feet away from our body, one could say that the eighth chakra is located on the edge of the fourth layer of one's aura. You might think about the eighth chakra as the file cabinet where all your karmic experiences are stored. Karmic experiences are those experiences that you did not master yet and that you have agreed to work on and heal in this lifetime. For example, you might have had several life times in which you failed to learn how to forgive, and you decided on this life time master this quality. To learn to forgive you have to have people around you that will hurt you, betrayal your trust, your love and so on. The eight chakra has the blue print of all the other time you fail to forgive until you learn to master this quality, the eight chakra, like a radar, will be sending messages to the world, searching and attracting those people whose vibration match our need to be hurt. It is like you were advertising to the world: "I need to learn how to forgive, please come and hurt me" to allow me to practice forgiveness. Every time we feel stuck, or we find ourselves repeating the same situation over and over again, it is indication that we are, through the eight chakra, attracting the right people and situations into our life so that we can re-experience the same situation, master it and grow from it. Many times, unaware of this, unaware of this process, we run away from people and or situations, only to find ourselves, later on, involved in identical situation.

A technique to clear the eight chakra is a very important part of the Integrated Energy Therapy® - IET training, not only to help the client master the karma activity, but also because is in the eight chakra that we carry the essence of our dream. Our specific soul's mission, in this lifetime. With the clearing of our eighth chakra we start to shed suppressed karmic energy that has been re-experienced in this lifetime and also release the divine spark of creativity that allows us to perceive our soul's mission and bring it to fruition.

Now that the reader is aware of how the chakras influence physical, mental and emotional states, and, indeed, also has a very strong influence on those around us, the question arises: How does one go about opening, balancing, cleansing, and developing one's chakras? Meditation is a great tool for enhancing the seven chakras: Meditation takes one to higher levels of consciousness and, consequently, to an improved understanding of the surrounding world. In view of the fact that this book concerns the role of the chakras in healing, I will not further dwell upon meditation. A quick search in the internet will bring to you several methods and ways to meditate.

Consider, also, returning to the descriptions of the negative qualities governed by each of the seven chakras. Make a list of those negative qualities, which you believe that you possess. Do not fight them; rather, acknowledge them. Realize that those negative qualities reside on the personality level, not on the spiritual level, because one's spiritual nature is pure, angelic, and perfect as God meant for us to be. Everything that is on the personality level can be changed by willpower. Ask your guardian angel to help you in the process of transformation, in the process of inner renovation. You will be amazed with the results.

Chakras open when we open up emotionally, when we rid ourselves of fear, and when we abandon judgment of others, situations and beliefs. Moreover, our energy centers open when we learn to accept things the way they truly are, when we come to understand that, as eternal spiritual beings, our main reason for this physical existence is to enhance our capacity for giving and receiving unconditional love.

Since Einstein demonstrated that we exist as a form of energy, it would be logical to view human emotions as energetic. Our thoughts (which we now know are energy) become our belief systems. Our belief systems influence all aspects of our mental, emotional, and physical health. It is our responsibility to guard our thoughts and to take charge of them. Only then can we be co-creators of a Universe of Love and Light. The first belief, which requires modification, is that we are physical beings occasionally having spiritual experiences. To the contrary, we are spiritual beings having a temporary physical experience. We must come to accept the truth that we are forms of pure energy.

Spiritual growth is available to all of us. Tools abound to help us gain knowledge and wisdom, in the form of books, videos, seminars and so forth.

For those who have already traveled some distance on the path to spiritual enlightenment, already mastering the complexities of the chakra system, I would recommend yet another step toward mastering subtle energy: learn to develop your *Light Body*.

THE LIGHT BODY

The light body is an energy body that exists at a higher level, closer to your soul than the chakras. The light body is composed of seven, vibrational, energy-body centers and three light-body centers.

By awakening the first-three energy-body centers, one can regulate the amount of energy one takes in from the environment, change less harmonious energies into harmonious oscillations, and utilize all ambient energy in one's immediate surroundings to develop higher consciousness. The first-three, vibrational energy-body centers form the power base of one's light body: working with these latter centers will provide a stronger sense of personal power, and enhance one's ability to remain centered, thereby releasing blocked emotional energy.

The upper-four, vibrational energy-body centers create flow and harmony, and take one to higher mental realms and other dimensions that are beyond time and space. Working with these centers, one can add light to his (or her) thoughts and open one's channel to the higher dimensions. One can experience many expanded states of awareness, which can feel deeply insightful, and, indeed, blissful. In such a state of expanded awareness, one may become transported beyond thought to new and different states of being.

Awaken the light-body centers, and *you* become a source of light; in so doing, you connect with your soul—increasing the balance, clarity, and harmony in your life. Awakening your light body is like having a new kind of vision: a form of vision whereby one can see, feel, or otherwise sense the higher, more beautiful energies of the soul plane—as well as one's own soul. Most importantly, these higher energetic views become an enriching component of one's daily living.

Awakening the light-body centers will improve your healing skills by facilitating the transmission of healing energy to those in need. You can more easily direct how you choose to feel, the thoughts you choose to think, and the healing environment you choose to provide to others.

Awakening your light body can assist you in gaining a clearer vision of your soul purpose, lifting the veils that shroud spirituality from physicality. Awakening the light body is a marvelous spiritual experience. It will bring light to everything you think or do. However, the process of awakening the light body cannot be learned by simply reading a book: the student of light body arousal will require a period of apprenticeship, or instruction, by an experienced teacher; a teacher trained to transmit the vibrational energy sounds, which correspond to each of the vibrational energy-body centers of the light body.

The light body classes were developed by spiritual guides, DaBen and Orin, and are taught by Duane Packer and Sanaya Roman (enrollment information for classes in light body may be found at the following web site: http://www. orindaben.com. Awakening one's light body will assist the prospective healer's work in *any* system energy healing.

HEALING HANDS

The Laying-on of Hands

Healers' hands have been said to drive off disease, to rejuvenate old and crippled bodies, and to restore the ailing to life and happiness. If true, the list of maladies that have been or can be cured by healing touch is astonishing: arthritis, asthma, bursitis, cancer, cataracts, cerebral palsy, epilepsy, gallstones, heart disease, paralysis, tuberculosis, vertigo, and tooth decay—to name a few. In some cases, physical contact appears not to be necessary. Many healers practice at a distance, finding that a client's belief in the inner healing capacity of the self is often sufficient to banish illness; these practitioners have dispensed with touch entirely.

Exploring the many different modalities of spiritual healing is an exhilarating process of self-teaching and concomitant inner growth. When we think that we have become aware of everything that is available, we soon discover that there is much more to explore: There are many teachers, providing instruction in truly wonderful healing techniques; indeed, both prospective healers and their clients-to-be may take encouragement from this latter statement of fact.

We are all aware that one's hands outstretched, to counteract another's pain with comforting touch, is a universal human act. A mother's soothing palm and comforting kiss can do wonders for a child's fevered brow or a painful bruise. Indeed, a friendly arm around a harried colleague's shoulder may ease a splitting headache in the work place. Of late, an increasing number of researchers are coming to realize that the therapeutic effect of touch goes far beyond mere gestures of comfort.

From the earliest days of human history, the laying-on of hands to affect a cure has been accepted by many societies as a natural means of healing. Legend and history, as well today's news, abound with descriptions of healers who seem to possess supernormal powers of touch, persons whose hands can alleviate severe symptoms and remedy complex medical conditions.

SUBTLE ENERGY—THE COMMON DENOMINATOR

Through the years, I have searched for the secret of healing through the laying-on of hands. Seemingly an enigmatic process, I have attended many lectures on healing, always anticipating that someone would finally disclose the perfect technique. Was there a special ritual? Was there certain format? Maybe there is a perfect way to place one's hands?

Although all that I have learned has aided my practice, I have come to conclude that healing energy, is wholly complete—it does not require a special technique, in order to work. Whatever you call that greater power, which you recognize as greater than yourself—Creator, Divinity, God, Goddess, Higher Power, Allah, Brahma, Buddha or Love—that power will work through you, to direct healing energy where it is needed.

Assuming that you have love in your heart and a strong unselfish desire to help others, healing energy will follow your intent: that is why knowledge of human anatomy and knowledge of the subtle energy body tremendously aids the practice of healing.

In the following chapter, I will share with the readers my personal limited knowledge of a number of well-known healing techniques. This knowledge was hard won: acquired through years of study, and research on two different continents. However, it is my fervent hope that first-hand application of such hard won knowledge provokes the reader to realize that the universal energy; available to each one of us, is the fundamental mechanism behind hands-on healing.

Although the techniques of hands-on healing vary tremendously from one methodology to another; indeed, from one practitioner to another, there is one common denominator to all hands-on practices: healing is accomplished through the directed flow of subtle energy.

It does not matter how the practitioner describes the subtle energy: The *Vedic* view refers to the chakras as energy points; other methods refer to *pranayama* (the power of breath). Prana is a Sanskrit word literally meaning the "life-force," the invisible bio-energy or vital energy that keeps the body alive and maintains a state of good health. The Japanese call this exact subtle energy, *Ki;* the Chinese describe it as *Chi;* while the Greeks refer to it as *Pneuma.* In Polynesian it is known as *Mana;* and in Hebrew, *Ruach*—meaning, "Breath of Life." All of the foregoing denominators refer to the same life force: It is subtle universal energy.

ENERGY HEALING

Despite the fact that I have chosen to limit my discussion of hands-on healing methods, I mean no disrespect to those healers who go about their valuable work, without following any of the described techniques. Among these healers are: Bradford (1996) who, by using the special technique of passing his hands around the client's body, accesses the client's energy centers; whereby, the client's subtle body is cleansed, balanced, and revitalized, Gawain (1979) teaches step-by-step techniques for self-healing.

In addition to citing the above-named healers, I mean to honor all healers that, absent any formal methodology, are giving to humanity the greatest gift of all: healing through love.

Pranic Healing

Pranic healing works by correcting imbalances in the energy field of the body. These imbalances are a reflection of physical, emotional and mental disorders. A pranic healer reinstates a person's physical, emotional and mental health, without touch, by applying appropriate frequencies of energy to specific areas of the body.

Scientific evidence provides tangible proof of the existence of the energy body and its relationship to the health and well-being of the physical body. Scientific experiments conducted by Semyon Kirlian, the eminent Russian scientist, using an ultra-sensitive photographic process (now known as Kirlian photography), showed a colorful, radiant energy field surrounding the physical bodies of humans, animals and plants (Roman, 1998). Moreover, experiments in Kirlian photography have also revealed that disease states appear first in the *energy body*, before manifesting themselves as an ailment of the physical body.

Pranic healing uses three basic techniques to correct disease-producing, energy imbalances: (a) scanning for energetic abnormalities caused by negative, used, or diseased energies; (b) removing abnormal energies; and (c) replenishing the energy body with vital energy. Pranic healing also involves increasing the practitioner's power to heal; protecting the client against contamination and adverse energies; strengthening the client's physical, emotional, and mental health; increasing the client's vitality and power; preventing diseases; improving the client's confidence to materialize goals; deepening the client's intuition, compassion, and peacefulness; and raising spiritual power safely for those who are interested in their spiritual development.

Pranic healing is taught at three levels, normally in one-day seminars.

Level 1. There are no prerequisites for enrollment in Level 1. Level 1 provides instruction in the connection between physical anatomy and the human energy system; how to increase the sensitivity of one's hands for scanning (sensing the energy level and corresponding condition) the aura and chakras; step-by-step techniques for healing energy abnormalities underlying over 90 diseases; techniques for self-healing and distance healing; and the ethics and responsibilities of pranic healing.

Level 2. The prerequisite for enrollment in Level 2 is satisfactory completion of a Level 1 seminar in pranic healing. Level 2 further develops the ability to scan, interpret, and treat energy imbalances by using a variety of frequencies for specific ailments. Level 2 instruction provides: detailed methods to work with more serious diseases; techniques to stimulate the immune system, cleanse the blood and internal organs; methods of cell regeneration, for the rapid healing of fresh wounds and the reprogramming of diseased cells; techniques for rapid recovery and vitality; and further instruction in pranic ethics and responsibilities.

Level 3. The prerequisite for enrollment in Level 3 is satisfactory completion of a Level 2 seminar. Level 3 provides instruction in advanced techniques for healing compulsions, obsessions, addictions, depression, suicidal tendencies, phobias, trauma, irritability, violent behaviors, paranoia, and hallucinations; offers detailed procedures to combat alcohol and drug abuse; includes ways to clean adverse energies from foods, pets, homes, and objects; provides instructions for disintegrating or transmuting negative psychic energies; teaches methods for repairing holes, cracks, and other damage to charkas; and provides advanced instruction in pranic ethics and responsibilities.

Pranic healing is currently being taught to physicians, nurses, massage therapists, acupuncturists, chiropractors, the clergy, homemakers, engineers, and many others—in all walks of life. Pranic healing techniques have enabled these latter individuals to heal confidently and consistently, in the shortest learning time possible.

Some physicians, like Eric Robins, M.D. (a Board Certified Urologist, practicing in Los Angeles, California), found that incorporating pranic healing into their medical practice aids the recovery of their clients. Robins (1999) makes the following statement: "I have been using Pranic Healing in my standard medical practice for almost a year. It has been used to effectively treat migraine headaches, Labyrinthitis [inflammation of the inner ear], chronic bladder pain, menstrual cramps, anxiety, insomnia, irritable bowel syndrome, and musculoskeletal problems. It has worked well on postoperative clients to help return of bowel function, and return to feeling "normal" again. It has proven to be an excellent complement to my standard practice of allopathic medicine."

Therapeutic Touch

Therapeutic Touch (TT) was developed by Dolores Krieger, Ph.D., R.N. (Professor Emeritus, New York University) and her mentor, Dora Kunz, in the early 1970s. Krieger (1979); notes that TT is now supported by major nursing organizations such as the National League of Nurses and the American Nursing Association. The North American Nursing Diagnostic Association now lists *energy-field disturbance* as a nursing diagnosis.

Since its start, TT has grown rapidly. It is currently practiced in over 80 hospitals in North America. It is taught in over 100 locations in 75 countries. More than 100,000 individuals have been taught the method; this number includes at least 43,000 health-care professionals. TT has been the subject of numerous doctoral dissertations and masters theses; and in early 1994, the (U.S.) National Institute of Health awarded a research grant to study TT. More than any other laying-on-of-hands technique, TT has reaped the respect and interest of the medical community.

TT is based upon the theory that there is a universal life energy that sustains all living organisms. In a healthy body, life-energy flows freely in, through and out of the organism, in a balanced manner, nourishing all the organs of the body. In disease, the flow of vital energy is obstructed, disordered, and depleted.

The energy field outside of the body generates an aura. Many believe that the aura extends outwards from the skin for a distance of 4 to 8 inches (10 to 20 cm). Others feel that the aura is only the first layer of the energy field, and that the field extends about 3 feet (1 m) in all directions from the body. Brennan (1987); reports that the subtle body; is seen as having seven layers. TT healers work with these subtle body layers.

TT practitioners, having learned to attune to the universal field, direct life-energy into clients to enhance their vitality. TT practitioners also help clients assimilate vital energy by releasing congestion, and balancing areas where the flow of energy has become disordered. Inasmuch as the TT practitioner draws upon the universal field, he (or she) does not become drained of his (or her) own energy; rather, he (or she) is continuously replenished therefrom.

Since the localized field of the client penetrates and extends beyond the body, actual physical contact is not necessary for TT treatment. In the jargon of Therapeutic Touch; healing means, helping the client to re-establish an open, balanced energy flow.

TT treatment is composed of: (a) assessing the quality of the person's energy—searching for areas of energetic congestion, disorder and deficit; (b) clearing congestion; (c) transferring life-energy into depleted areas; and (d) balancing the flow of vital energy.

Treatment of disease Using, Therapeutic Touch.

The TT practitioner will center himself (or herself) in a calm and focused state, to quiet his (or her) mind and emotions, through a prayer or brief meditation. After centering himself (or herself); and, having the client seated on a stool, or sideways on a chair, so that the client's back is unobstructed, the practitioner is ready to proceed with the first phase of treatment.

The first phase of TT treatment is the *assessment*: The practitioner will gently pass his (or her) hands over the surface of the client's body, maintaining a distance from the surface of the skin which ranges from three to five inches (7.5 to 12.5 cm), palms facing the body, starting from the top of the head and moving down to the feet: when the hand in back reaches the vicinity of client's hips, the practitioner keeps it there while the other hand is passed all the way down the legs to the feet. During this process the TT practitioner will look for: (a) *loose congestion* (loose congestion feels like a cloud or a wave of heat, thickness, pressure or heaviness; for example, if a person has a wound or an infection, loose congestion can often be found around this area), (b) *tight congestion* (tight congestion might feel like an area of coldness or emptiness—for example, if the TT practitioner is assessing a client with ulcerative colitis, a sensation of coldness or emptiness will be felt around the client's intestinal area— it is well to observe that individuals with chronic problems generally suffer from energy blockage), (c) *deficit* (considering that illness is always associated with depletion of vital energy, the deficit is most easily perceived around a problem area, such as the site of a wound or infection; the TT practitioner probably will experience the energy deficit as a drawing or pulling sensation—perhaps as a feeling of hollowness), and (d) *imbalance* (energetic imbalance will be felt in different ways—as static electricity or a prickly, tingly, "pins and needles" sensation—uncomfortable to the practitioner hands; alternatively, the energy may seem to flap or surge, in and out, in a disorganized manner).

Most importantly, the prospective healer must remain aware that assessment cues obtained during the first phase of TT treatment are not sharply delineated; rather, they are blurred, tending to overlap one another.

The second phase of TT treatment is *clearing congestion*. Energy congestion normally travels from the head downward; congestion is easily cleared from the client's energy body with gradual, repetitive, downward-sweeping motions of the hands.

The third phase of TT treatment is *transferring life-energy into depleted areas:* The TT practitioner will consciously establish the intent to become a conduit for the universal Life force. (The intent to serve as a *device* for energy conduction is of utmost importance; otherwise the practitioner will inadvertently transfer his or her own energy to the client and subsequently become depleted.) To direct the life-energy to the client, many practitioners use visualization; e.g., a stream of light coming from above, flowing through oneself, and thence entering the client. The practitioner may then direct his (or her) hands to the problem areas, transferring life-energy to them. Inner guidance and experience alert the healer when it is time to move from one area to another.

The fourth and final phase of TT treatment is *balancing energy flow*. In consequence of the fact that bodily disease is a manifestation of disturbance in the subtle energy body, the TT practitioner will end treatment by balancing the entire energy field with feather-like movements over the entire body, from head to toe.

The Relaxation Response

Benson (1996) has used relaxation response (RR) with great success, to relieve pain and treat chronically ill clients. RR is an easy-to-perform, do-it-yourself healing method. The client is invited to choose a word, prayer or phrase that has a personally soothing effect. He (or she) then repeats the word(s) or phrase for about 20 minutes, passively disregarding everyday thoughts that come to mind during the repetition. Benson notes that the hallmark feature of RR is a significant decrease in the body's oxygen consumption, or *hypo metabolism*.

The oxygen in the air which one breathes is used by the body's cells to burn the nutrients from the food one consumes: this bodily function is called metabolism. During the practice of RR, the body decelerates metabolism, allowing one's internal organs to reduce the pace of bodily activity. The need for fuel to sustain the body is greatly reduced. The heart need not beat so rapidly (relaxed muscles require less blood flow), and breathing can be slowed and deepened.

Let's compare the relaxation response to the physical opposite: the fight-or-flight response. The fight-or-flight response rapidly and involuntarily increases the body's oxygen consumption (fast breathing), accelerates cardiac output (strong, rapid heartbeat), and increases the body's metabolic rate (caloric output) to provide nutrient energy in preparation for the violent muscular activity of fighting or fleeing: indeed, the body enters a state of *hypermetabolic* activity.

In view of the above discussion, it is easy to understand the value of RR. Moreover, the relaxation response operates, whether you believe in it or not. Clients with terminal cancer have successfully eased pain with RR, as have others who suffer from chronically recurring pain, e.g., migraine. Clients who suffer from migraine headaches have reported that, after a few weeks of practicing the RR twice a day (and for a moment or two—at the first twinge of a headache), they were able to shorten the time between headaches. Later, these latter clients were able to reduce the severity of the headache pain; and some reported that, within a few months, the migraine headaches had disappeared entirely.

Chigong -The Skill Of Attracting Vital Energy

Chigong is a term of art to be found in Chinese medicine, which is derived from its constituent parts: *Chi* (Chi), or energy, and *Gong* (Kung), or skill. It is properly pronounced, "chee-gong."

The practice of Chigong dates back at least two thousand years. *Many* ancient cultures believed that preternatural or, indeed, physical "energy flow" regulated the functioning of their bodies and of the world around them. In China, manipulation of this energy flow to improve health was gradually formalized in such medical disciplines as acupuncture, acupressure, and Chigong.

The philosophical foundations of Chigong stipulate that the vital energy, *chi*, flows along meridians that link the internal organs with the fingers or toes, and more than 100 acupuncture points on the head, spine and other parts of the body. It's believed that illness results from an imbalance of *chi*, when more accumulates in one place than another. The meditation, visualization, breathing, and movement exercises of Chigong seek to restore balance, break down blockages to the flow of *chi*, and reestablish a healthy supply of vital energy to the diseased or distressed parts of the body.

Although *chi*, itself, is undetectable, modern proponents of traditional Chinese medicine maintain that manipulating this force with Chigong results in a variety of physical benefits, including reductions in heart rate and blood pressure, dilation of the blood vessels, and enhanced oxygenation of the tissues. The exercises are said to have a beneficial effect on the nerves that regulate the pain response. By increasing the flow of lymphatic fluid, Chigong practices are thought to improve the efficiency of the immune system. And by improving circulation, they are said to speed elimination of toxic substances from the body, improving general health.

Some practitioners claim that Chigong moderates the function of the hypothalamus, pituitary, and pineal glands—as well as the meningeal fluid surrounding the brain and spinal cord—to decrease pain, increase immunity, and improve mood. Others say that it increases the number of disease-fighting, white blood cells, promotes the production of enzymes and other substances needed for digestion, and improves blood oxygen saturation by increasing the lungs' *capacity* to absorb this vital gas.

While such effects could indeed promote better health, Western critics demand scientific proof that they actually occur. These latter skeptics would also like to see definitive proof that Chigong has actually cured illness. Although there are many Chinese studies that seem to prove the power of Chigong, the ancient practice has never been subjected to the rigorous tests of efficacy that Western therapies routinely undergo. (In such "double-blind" trials, a treatment must measurably outperform a placebo control; moreover, neither the clients nor the clinician performing the study know whom receives the treatment and whom receives the placebo.)

Although the curative power of Chigong remains to be proved to Western medical scientists, even critics of Chigong admit that it can enhance fitness and promote healthy relaxation. And, though their reasons remain a mystery, many conventional physicians in the United States admit that they have treated clients whose health has improved after the practice of Chigong.

Chigong is a self-healing art that combines movement and meditation. Visualizations are employed to enhance the mind/body connection and assist healing. Regular practice of Chigong can prevent and treat illness; reduce stress and anxiety; combat insomnia; relieve certain types of headache; improve physical fitness, balance, and flexibility; integrate mind, body, and spirit; and bring about inner peace.

In traditional Chinese medicine, however, a form of Chigong—known as *external* Chigong—is credited with much more. Proponents of external Chigong claim that it has cured cancer, heart disease, AIDS, arthritis, and asthma. They also recommend it for migraines, hemorrhoids, constipation, diabetes, high blood pressure, menstrual problems, prostate trouble, impotence, and pain. Some say it even corrects nearsightedness and farsightedness. The practice of external Chigong is almost impossible to find in the U.S.

However, instruction in internal Chigong is widely available. There are at least 3,000 variations, ranging from simple movements that coordinate breathing and calisthenics, to complex exercises aimed at altering such vital bodily functions as heart rate and brain wave frequency. Internal Chigong can be practiced by anyone: healthy or sick, young or old. The exercises, which are easily adapted to one's physical abilities, can be performed walking, standing, sitting in a wheelchair, or even lying down—if necessary.

One can teach himself (or herself) Chigong by following instructions in the many training manuals available in bookstores and libraries. Videotapes are also available for those who want to become self-taught. However, many experts warn that, even though the exercises seem simple, it's wise to start with professional instruction, either one-on-one, or in a group. Classes are frequently offered at local YMCAs, community fitness centers, and hospitals.

Wear loose, comfortable clothing and flexible shoes when you exercise. Do not eat or drink anything, especially alcoholic beverages, within 90 minutes of your Chigong sessions. Some practitioners suggest that you avoid sexual intercourse for at least one hour before and one hour after exercising; others don't seem to think this latter proscription is necessary.

It is important to approach Chigong with an optimistic attitude, proponents say. It is also important to try to do your best, even if it seems difficult. For example, if you are told to hold your breath, hold it as long as possible. If you are supposed to remain in one position, remain in position for as long as you can. If your arm or leg cannot be maintained in the required position, let it fall naturally. If you find you cannot follow all three aspects of an exercise—visualizing, moving, and breathing—at the same time, concentrate first on visualization.

Chigong exercises can be performed in any order. Repeat each one 6 times when you begin, and increase the number of repetitions when you feel you are ready. Do not rush, and do not expect immediate results. Your Chigong instructor will begin with simple movements. To attain the greatest benefit, you must follow his (or her) instructions exactly. The *opening position* prepares your mind and body to enter a *Chigong state*. The remainder of the exercise (moving and breathing) is supposed to stimulate the flow of *chi*. You may be asked to stand with your legs apart and breathe from the diaphragm while you move your arms and legs in a specific way. Or you may have to sit and roll objects between your palms, or simply walk slowly. You may also be taught meditation techniques. Here are a few typical exercises:

Child worships the Buddha. The Chigong exercise, child worships the Buddha, is said to strengthen the legs, lighten the body, and relieve stress. The exercise is performed as follows: (a) standing with legs apart, open your arms and inhale deeply; (b) bring your hands together, directly in front of you, and raise your left leg; (c) from the previously raised position, rest your left leg on your right knee, breathe out, and, at the same time, gently bend your right leg; and (d) hold the position—then return to the starting position and repeat.

<u>Directing vital life energy to internal organs.</u> This latter Chigong exercise is performed as follows: (a) rub your hands together; (b) place your right hand on the lower right edge of your rib cage (the vicinity of the liver), while you visualize your liver receiving *chi;* (c) place your left hand on the lower left side of your ribs (the area of the spleen and pancreas), while visualizing these organs receiving *chi*; (d) move your emplaced hands in a circle, while breathing deeply and relaxing—try to feel heat energy *inwardly* conducted through the surface of your skin, penetrating these organs, and making them work more efficiently; (e) hold your hands over the described organs and continue feeling the heat; (f) exhale, while visualizing *chi* circulating from the center of your body to your arms and hands and then into other organs; (g) move your palms to cover your naval and breastbone—rub your naval and breastbone—and, as you rub them, visualize the *chi* pouring into your naval, heart, and thymus, improving their functioning; and (h) move your palms to your lower back and rub the area—visualize your kidneys and adrenals receiving *chi,* thereby improving their functioning.

<u>Breathing to increase energy.</u> In order to perform this latter exercise, proceed as follows: (a) sit (or stand) with eyes closed or slightly open, shoulders relaxed, head centered above shoulders, and hands palm-up with fingertips pointing toward each other—held approximately two inches (5 cm) below your navel; (b) as you slowly breathe in, raise your hands to the lower edge of your breastbone—take three short puffs of breath to fill your lungs, raising your hands with each puff until they reach the level of your armpits & hold; (c) turn your palms face-down—lower your hands to your navel while exhaling slowly—exhale three additional puffs to empty your lungs & hold again; and (d) as you inhale, visualize the *chi* gathering inside your pelvic and abdominal cavities—continue visualizing as you exhale.

<u>Spontaneous movement</u>: Is a Chigong exercise said to produce an immediate sensation of *chi.* The exercise is conducted in this manner: (a) stand with your feet apart or sit in an armless chair; (b) wiggle your

fingers, shake and rock your body; (c) breathing more deeply, shake your arms, then your head, and finally your shoulders; (d) relaxing your jaw, sigh or make another sound as you exhale; and (e) exaggerate or prolong the movements, shift your weight from foot to foot, make more sounds—make up your own routine.

The *external* form of Chigong, as practiced in China, requires none of the foregoing activities. Instead, a Chigong master, endowed with plentiful *chi*, imparts the vital force to the client. To transmit the *chi*, the master may wave his hands above the person's body, touch him, or press down on specific points. The supplemental *chi* is said to balance the client's own life force, thus promoting healing.

In China, such masters have their own medical association, and many hospitals use their services for routine treatment. In the early 1980s, Lu Yan Fang, a Beijing scientist, discovered that the hands of masters emitted low frequency sound waves that were 100 times more powerful than those of normal people, and 1,000 times stronger than the elderly or ill. She then built a machine (the Infratonic QGM) to replicate these sounds, and found that they seemed to reduce pain. Today, the Infratonic QGM is used in the Far East, parts of Europe, Mexico, and Argentina. In the U.S., the Infratonic QGM is available as an FDA-approved *massage device* that is frequently used to treat pain. The interested reader is referred to the China Healthways Institute (CHI) for further information; the institute's web address is http://www.exo.com/~chi.

Contraindications for Chigong therapy. Because Chigong therapy increases circulation—and, thereby, may thin the blood—one should forgo Chigong exercises during periods when bleeding could become a problem, e.g., after a tooth extraction, bodily trauma, or when suffering from internal bleeding. The exercises should also be suspended during pregnancy. And it's best to avoid Chigong exercises completely, if you have a tendency to vertigo or are suffering a severe mental or emotional disturbance.

Craniosacral Therapy

Craniosacral therapists recognize health as an active principle. Health is viewed as an expression of life, an inherently ordering force, and a natural internal intelligence. Craniosacral Therapy (CT) is a subtle, profound healing modality that assists natural bodily intelligence. It is clear that the living human organism is immensely complex, requiring an enormous amount of internal organization: CT helps to nurture the internal ordering principles. CT increases physical vitality and well-being, not only by effecting structural change, but also by affecting mental and emotional health—with wider implications; e.g., improved interpersonal relationships, ability to manage more appropriately, etc.

Dr. William Sutherland, an American osteopath, discovered the *intrinsic movements* of the bones of the skull around the turn of the century. His further research revealed rhythmic tidal motions in the body. These movements, which can be measured with delicate scientific instruments, are a direct expression of the health of the client.

As research continued, it became apparent that these various movements are inextricably linked with not only physical health, but also with mental and emotional health. Palpation of these tide-like motions permits craniosacral therapists to facilitate change in areas of restriction. Most notably, *restriction of movement* corresponds to an *inability* of the life force to actuate the body's mechanism for self-healing. This latter absence of health may result in disease, malaise, or numbness.

CT is a gentle, non-invasive, highly effective form of therapy. Seldom does the therapist use more than five grams of pressure (the weight of a nickel). The healing work can be profoundly relaxing, exhilarating, deeply moving, or precipitate the resolution of repressed issues. Sometimes the benefits of CT are not immediately noticeable, but become obvious on returning to a familiar environment.

<u>The craniosacral system</u>: The craniosacral system consists of the tissues,

membranes, and the fluid, that surrounds and supports the brain and spinal cord. It extends from the bones of the head (cranium) down to the bones at the base of the spine (sacrum). The fluid within the membranes is continuously draining and refilling.

The cyclical filling and draining of meningeal fluid creates gentle, rhythmic, expanding-and-contracting movements that can be felt anywhere in the body by a trained Craniosacral therapist. These latter movements constitute the craniosacral rhythm. They occur at a rate of about six to twelve complete cycles per minute.

The therapist gains valuable information about where the body would most benefit from therapy by monitoring the craniosacral rhythm: The source of pain isn't always obvious.

CT is helpful for people of all ages. It has successfully been used to treat such diverse conditions as headache, chronic infections of the middle ear, vertigo, depression, back pain, joint immobility, neck pain, sinus congestion, migraines, learning disabilities, aftereffects of childhood trauma, and negative touch.

In infants, CT is used to treat colic; sleep disorders; feeding problems; breathing or digestive difficulties; various congenital, neurological and genetic problems; and the aftereffects of forceps, vacuum extractor or cesarean delivery.

CT treatment proceeds as follows: The client rests fully clothed on a massage table, while the therapist monitors the *craniosacral rhythm* with his (or her) hands. The CT practitioner performs other assessments, and corrects the sources of pain and dysfunction using gentle manipulative techniques. This therapeutic activity permits the body to most efficiently use its own power to heal. Because the body expends considerable energy to adapt to its restrictions, most people find the therapeutic sessions to be deeply relaxing. Formerly inhibited emotions rise to the surface and are released. After receiving CT, clients report greater clarity, peacefulness, and insight—along with profound relief from their physical symptoms.

To become a craniosacral therapist, an average of 500 hours of training are required, which includes hundreds of hours of hands-on practice. (http://www.craniosacraltherapy.org)

Reiki

Reiki is a Japanese word that combines two elemental terms, *Rei* (universal) and *Ki* (life-force). *Ki* is the Japanese variant of the Chinese word; *Chi* Reiki is the modern version of a more ancient method of spiritual attunement, attained through the laying-on of hands.

<u>Reiki in historical perspective</u> - Reiki was originated in Japan, in the middle 1850's, by Dr. Mikao Usui, dean of a small Christian university in Kyoto. During this period, Japan was greedily adopting philosophies and technologies that were being introduced by Western diplomats, businessmen, and Christian missionaries. Japan was rapidly becoming an industrial and military giant rivaling many nations in the West.

Dr. Usui had become a Christian through religious conversion by Western missionaries. He faced his greatest academic challenge (and personal crisis of faith) during a discussion with his students: he was asked if he *literally* believed the Bible.

Dr. Usui replied in the affirmative, a student asked him about the healings that Jesus performed, and further asked why they were not being performed to the present day. Continuing to question the raising of the dead and the healing of the sick, the student quoted Jesus' New Testament assertion, "You will do as I have done, and even greater things": If all this is true the students said, please teach us how to do it. Dr. Usui was stunned that he was *unable* to reconcile his inability to answer his students with his primary obligation to teach. He resigned his academic position on that very day.

Dr. Usui was determined, however, to discover the answers that he had been unable to provide to his former students. He traveled to America and began his research at the University of Chicago Theological Seminary. After a period of study, and still unable to find the necessary answers, he returned to Japan to study the teachings of Buddha who also had been able to heal.

Approached by Dr. Usui, abbots of various Buddhist monasteries explained that although they were aware of Buddha's physical healing skills, present day focus was on the healing of spirit. He came to a Zen monastery, where for the first time, an abbot encouraged his research by responding that whatever was possible at one time, could be accomplished again.

Dr. Usui was greatly encouraged by the abbot's words; he remained at the monastery and began a study of the *Sutras* in Japanese. Later, he studied Chinese and Tibetan *Sutras* in Sanskrit. After completing his study of the Tibetan *Lotus Sutra*, he felt that he had found the answer for which he had so long searched. Believing that he had found the key to healing, he returned to the Zen abbot and asked his advice on how to receive the needed empowerment. After a period of meditation, the abbot suggested that Dr. Usui should go to Mount Kuri Yama, about 17 miles (27 km) from Kyoto, and commence a 21-day fast and meditation.

Dr. Usui journeyed to the mountain, located a spot facing east, and gathered a pile of 21 stones, which he would use as a calendar. He fasted and meditated for 20 days without success. Early in the morning of the 21st day, there was great darkness all around him. Suddenly in the darkness appeared a sparkle of light that began to grow larger and larger and rushed toward him. Usui became frightened and had the urge to rise up and run away, but he was unable to move. He braced himself for impact as the intense light struck him in the middle of his forehead. He thought he was dying. Millions of rainbow-colored bubbles appeared around him and suddenly turned into white glowing balls, each one containing a three-dimensional, golden Sanskrit character. When he had memorized each character he awoke from his trance and was surprised to find that he was in broad daylight.

He rushed down the mountain to inform the abbot of his success, when he tripped and stubbed his toe quite badly. Reaching down to grab it, he was amazed that the bleeding stopped and the pain subsided after a few minutes of cradling it. Dr. Usui then came to a roadside inn and ordered breakfast. The proprietor's granddaughter, who served Dr. Usui, was in great pain from a severe toothache. Dr. Usui offered to help the woman, and laid his Hands-on the sides of her face: her pain and swelling soon subsided.

Dr. Usui returned to the monastery and reported the preceding events to the abbot. At that time, however, the abbot was in great pain from a bout of arthritis; whereupon, Dr. Usui laid his Hands-on the arthritic areas, and the pain soon disappeared. The abbot was amazed, and encouraged Dr. Usui to continue his healing activity.

Soon thereafter, Dr. Usui started passing his healing gift to others; a ritual was created for this purpose; and it is what the today's *Reiki* call *attunement* or *initiation*. It is known that the Reiki symbols Dr. Usui received on Mount Kuri Yama are the symbols used today by Reiki masters, on the attunement of practitioners. (http://www.reiki-luso.com)

On becoming a Reiki practitioner: One cannot become a Reiki practitioner by reading a book, or by listening to an audiotape. To become *energy sensitive,* one must be attuned by an experienced Reiki master, through a series of initiations, which prepares the prospective practitioner for three levels of service in the Healing Arts.

The purpose of initiation is to attune the new practitioner, so that his (or her) body can channel the new energy. The energy, once the body is attuned, will flow into the *crown chakra* and can be felt in one's hands.

The energy can also be felt in one's feet; indeed, healing could be accomplished by the practitioner placing his (or her) feet upon the client. It is more practical, however, for most practitioners to use their hands to channel energy; however, in cases of disability, the practitioner may not be able to use his (or her) hands.

Initiation into the practice of Reiki: Initiation or *attunement* of the prospective Reiki practitioner is accomplished through three levels of instruction. In the *first attunement* (Reiki I), the initiate receives the first healing symbol: the symbol of the *heart chakra*, the subtle energy center for receiving and focusing healing energy. The first attunement also introduces the individual to the spiritual community and pairs him (or her) with a Reiki master from the *inner planes.* Through ritual performed by the Reiki master, the initiate is infused with the divine chakra symbol, and is empowered by the received symbol to heal others and himself (or herself). Techniques for laying-on hands are also taught at this level. After the first attunement, the practitioner is then able to apply Reiki energy treatment to others and to himself (or herself).

The *second attunement* (Reiki II) draws the initiate deeper into spiritual service. Here the individual is given the second healing symbol: the symbol of the *throat chakra*, called lightning and thunder. Here the individual is taught the method for distance healing using the received symbols of Reiki I and II. In addition, the initiate is taught the art of *quick healing,* primarily used in emergency situations. Here too, through ritual, the initiate is infused with the divine symbol of the respective chakra—and he (or she) is accordingly empowered to heal others and himself (or herself).

In the final or *third attunement,* the initiate is given the third healing symbol, the *crown chakra*—again through ritual. Those who receive this final initiation are called *Reiki masters;* they may heal according to their calling, and they may initiate candidates into Reiki healing service.

Generally, all who seek the first attunement are accepted by their chosen Reiki master. However, a truly responsible master will give the next two initiations only to those who show aptitude and spiritual maturity: Reiki healing art is a deeply spiritual study; it is not meant for those who are not spiritual, or for those who do not demonstrate a degree of spiritual preparedness.

Reiki therapy: Typically, the client would expect to be placed on a massage table, fully clothed, for about 45-90 minutes. The practitioner will likely provide soft mood lighting (or candles) and, perhaps, play quiet background music—as an aid to induce the client to relax. The practitioner will rest his hands in *key* positions on the client's body, maintaining contact for about three to five minutes at each position. He (or she) will likely remain quiet during this time, to allow the client time for self-observation of the healing experience. Healing energy directed by Reiki practitioners often feels warm and soothing; for some, however, it can variously feel cool, tingly, thick, or heavy.

Many clients will notice that they become aware of sensations in their bodies in places other than the site occupied by the practitioner's hands. This common experience indicates that the healing energy, *chi*, is channeled to the location whereat the client's body is most in need. It is also not uncommon to have various colors spring to mind, or simply to become aware that the area behind your eyes is no longer black—but perhaps conveys colors, shapes, and/or other visual impressions. Reiki energy works on all levels of the body at the same time, not just the physical plane; therefore, it is also possible to experience an emotional reaction during a Reiki healing session.

In a traditional Reiki session, there is usually no manipulation of tissue; however, many practitioners—who are also skilled in massage and/or physical therapy—may combine massage with Reiki, in order to enhance both processes.

Practitioners will employ Reiki in a number of situations: allergies, behavioral modification, stress management, depression—even trauma and critical care. The Reiki practitioner may or may not have an extensive background in the study of anatomy; regardless, he (or she) will be able to work effectively toward healing goals established by the client. The Reiki practitioner serves as a *channel* for the universal life force; the practitioner is *not* the source of healing energy. Indeed, the practitioner is viewed as an extension of the client's natural healing abilities.

Reiki is gaining acceptance, in hospitals and clinics across America, as a meaningful and cost-effective way to improve client care. California Pacific Medical Center is one of the largest hospitals in Northern California. Its Health and Healing Clinic, a branch of the Institute for Health and Healing, provides care for both acute and chronic illnesses using a wide range of complementary methods, including Reiki, Chinese medicine, hypnosis, biofeedback, acupuncture, homeopathy, herbal therapy, nutritional therapy, and aromatherapy. The clinic features six treatment rooms and is currently staffed by two physicians, Drs. Mike Cantwell and Amy Saltzman. Cantwell, a pediatrician specializing in infectious diseases, is a Reiki master with training in nutritional therapy. Saltzman specializes in internal medicine, and has training in mindfulness meditation, acupuncture, and nutritional therapy.

Reiki methodologies: There are different frequencies of healing energy (sometimes referred to as *energy rays*) and, consequently, a given Reiki practitioner may be specifically attuned to one frequency or another. Which frequency is better? It is this writer's opinion that there is no such thing as better (or worse) energy. The universal life force is omnipresent; therefore, the truly significant assessment to be made is how *effectively* one uses it. Healing energy *always* follows intention; therefore, the practitioner's *intent* (directing and focusing ability) is of utmost importance.

As an example, one of the energy rays has been named as *Seichim*. It is the name for an energy healing and self-transformational system. *Seichim* was originally received by Patrick Zeigler, in 1980, while in Egypt. There are a variety of names used to describe this energy, and each healing methodology has a different means of accessing it. It is also known as *Sekhem, Seichem,* and *SKHM*. There are further variants, such as *Isis Seichim* and *Archangelic Seichim*. However, whether the healing energy is referred to as Seichim, Seichem, Sekhem, or SKHM, all are manifestations of *Living Light Energy.*

Other examples of Reiki methodology are the Karuna Reiki, which is a healing system founded by William Rand, following his discovery of new energy symbols; and Kathleen Milner's healing system, which became Tera Mai Reiki and Seichem. Milner's system is claimed to be "higher frequency" than Usui Reiki. Milner's system was formerly known as Sai Baba Reiki, but the name was changed due to legal complications arising from using the Sai Baba name. The system is trademarked, controlled, and regulated through the International Center for Reiki Studies (Michigan, USA). However, as with traditional Reiki, to perceive, manipulate and apply this *Living Light Energy,* attunement by a Reiki master is required. http://www.angelreiki.nu/seichim/)

Although there are many other valuable laying-on-of-hands techniques that deserve to be mentioned, I will close this chapter by describing a subtle-energy healing technique known as Integrated Energy Therapy – IET® - "Healing with the energy of the angels".

INTEGRATED ENERGY THERAPY (IET)®

IET is an energy therapy formulated by Stevan J. Thayer, a former electrical engineer. In 1984, Thayer resigned from his engineering career and redirected the focus of his life's work.

Soon thereafter, he completed a program of studies at the New Seminary, in New York City, and was ordained an Interfaith Minister. Further, he undertook various programs of study in holistic health therapies, culminating his training by becoming a Reiki Master. In his practice as a Reiki Master, he treated many clients who had energy blockages that Reiki alone did not clear. Today, Thayer is the founder and director of the Center of Being, in New York. He is a full time healer and teacher, and the channel for the angel Ariel.

While attempting to play a more active role in helping clients clear the afore-mentioned energy blockages, Thayer discovered the *cellular memory map* and the *energy integration points,* the conceptual bases of IET. Thayer has been teaching IET since 1994. The IET energy healing system is rapidly spreading not only in US, but also Australia, Belgium, Canada, Greece, The Netherlands, Ireland and Saudi Arabia. At the beginning of the year 2005 there were 1,100 IET Master Instructor and more than 16,000 IET practitioners. I had the privilege to be trained personally by Thayer in all levels of IET and became an IET Master Instructor in the year 2000. IET came to this writer's life in a very special way. It was during my first Light Body Seminar, taught by Sanaya Roman & Duane Packer, that I had my first mystical experience, in which an angel made his presence visible to me and talked to me. Among other things, the angel said: I am Ariel, I am the angel that brought you to this world, and I am the one that is going to be holding your hand on your way back home, but between birth and death, you have work do to. You are so far behind that I needed to come to alert you. For example, right now; you are supposed to be writing a book. Please get busy! I was amazed with the feeling of unconditional love that involved my being while I was in that presence. It is a feeling I will never forget, and also a feeling I was not able to duplicate since that Sunday in 1996. Back home, I gave some thoughts to the advice, but considering that English is my self-taught second language, writing a book seamed to a mountain too high to climb. On the other had the angel's advice/suggestion was too strong and clear to ignore. After considering all the possibilities, I decided to start writing in Portuguese (my first language) and I made it part of my daily spiritual practice for a few months. After a while, life demands and changes made me stop writing. It was in 1998 that I found a book written by Stevan Thayer "Interview with an angel" by angel Ariel. The angel's name compelled me to buy the book. What a surprise I had when I started reading that book. Not knowing, I was writing a Portuguese version of that book. I could not help but contact the author and share with him what had happened. Stevan then, shared with me that he had sold, the foreign rights for Interview with an Angel, to a South America publisher, and that the Portuguese version would be available in Brazil that year. In short: The angels wanted the book in Portuguese and they got it. After getting to know Stevan and his work, there was no doubt in my mind that since the angel's appearance, I was being guided to learn IET. Although I add several other healing modalities in my healing practice, IET is the main energy healing system in my practice. I hope the following descriptions of the IET method, will entice you too to learn this amazing and yet so simple to use, healing technique.

IET practitioners work within four levels of the human energy field: physical, emotional, mental and spiritual. As with other methods of healing through subtle energy, IET is a gentle, non-invasive way to restore health to the human energy field, the *aura* that surrounds and pervades the physical body. An IET practitioner will diagnose energy flow, treat the energy body and provide support to the client in many ways to promote healing and wellness at all levels. Practitioners have developed the ability to connect to the universal life force energy and bring it through their hands to provide therapeutic treatment for their clients. IET can be used alone, or as a perfect complement to many modern and holistic treatment methods.

Confronted with the stresses of everyday life, one can become energetically imbalanced, become ill, or become injured in some way. Energy blockages or imbalances in the *aura* may become manifested as psychological or emotional disorders. This gentle hand on therapy is clear, concise and very effective. As you become familiar with the Cellular Memory Map you will note the various primary emotions linked to the physical body. For example: The Top of the Head correlates with guilt, the Kidney area - fear, the liver would be anger and so on. To treat the client's various symptoms, the IET practitioner will work with the *cellular memory map* and the nine, *energy integration points*.

On becoming an IET practitioner: One cannot become an IET practitioner by reading a book, or by listening to an audiotape. To become *energy sensitive,* one must be attuned by an experienced IET master instructor, through a series of initiations, which prepares the prospective practitioner for three levels of service in the Healing Arts.

IET is currently being taught in three levels: Basic IET, Intermediate IET, and Advanced IET. Practitioners use a technique called angelic heartlink to connect with the angelic energy available in the universe. IET healers use the ancient science of *geomancy* to amplify and focus healing energy (the IET energy ray).

Basic IET - In the basic-level training class, the student receives attunement to the basic IET energy-ray that will empower him (or her) to energize and integrate cellular memory blocks. The prospective IET healer also will (a) learn the location and use of the IET, energy-integration power points; (b) receive an introduction to *energy anatomy and the cellular memory map; (c) increase his (or her) ability to be energy intuitive and to* read energy; and (d) complete training in basic IET self-healing and facilitated healing.

Intermediate IET – The intermediate-level training provides the student with (a) attunement to the intermediate IET energy-ray that empowers him (or her) to pull energy imprints out of the human energy field; (b) instruction in clearing energy imprints from past-life karma; (c) methods to esoterically dowse the human energy field; and (d) complete training in the Intermediate IET treatment process

Advanced IET - The advanced-level class is the final step in IET training. It provides the student with attunement to the advanced IET energy-ray, which unlocks the energy of his (or her) soul's purpose. Advanced IET also will provide the following instruction: (a) how to perform a soul star clearing, to vitalize the purpose of one's soul; (b) use of the bring-your-dream-alive clearing process; (c) use of the powerful energy wave technique; and (d) complete training in the Advanced IET treatment process.

IET Treatment - An IET healing session requires sixty to ninety minutes. The therapy is best accomplished with the client lying on a massage table. After entering into a meditative state, the practitioner makes a silent prayer of gratitude, and asks the angelic forces of the universe to guide and direct the healing session for the client's highest healing and highest good. Following meditation and prayer, the IET practitioner makes the angelic *heartlink* connection, and begins the process of hands-on healing.

One-by-one, the practitioner manually applies light pressure to the nine IET integration points on the client's body, channeling healing energy into those points, to vitalize and integrate the cellular memory blocks. The practitioner also will sense and locate energy blockages within the client by accessing the physical, emotional, mental and spiritual layers of the client's energy body. Using the pullout and release technique, the IET practitioner releases the energy blockages, which are afflicting the body. During IET, it is common for emotional responses to occur. The release of these latter emotions is a great aid in the healing process.

After energy blockages are released, the practitioner will imprint angelic energy into the IET integration points to nourish and balance these energy centers. In the last phase of the IET treatment, the practitioner will pass his (or her) hands over the client's body, head to toe, maintaining a 2-inch to 5-inch (5-12.5 cm) hand-to-bodily-surface separation; thereby, sealing the aura and grounding the client.

Literature on IET is not yet publicly available: the foregoing description of IET is based upon the writer's own training and personal experience. The interested reader is referred to the following web site, www.learniet.com.

SUMMARY AND CONCLUSIONS

We are living in a fast-paced, action-oriented, "just-do-it" period in time. Present-day information technology, which is continuously improved, brings the world to our fingertips. However, as we satisfy our collective appetite for improved information gathering, we also acquire an overwhelming amount of stress to continuously keep pace with the information that we have gathered.

We have come to enjoy less and less unstructured time for ourselves. In the daily press to survive — let alone excel—we feel crushed among our business responsibilities, familial obligations, and the need to relentlessly improve ourselves—in order to remain competitive.

It is no wonder why our moods shift many times, in any given day. We daily progress from joy to sadness; then, anger and frustration becomes directed toward others and ourselves, in an uncontrolled (and seemingly uncontrollable) cycle. This emotional roller coaster of business survival, familial obligation, time compression, poor nutrition, and peer pressure to "keep up" is jeopardizing our collective physical health.

Meanwhile, medical science is spending hundreds of millions of healthcare dollars on epidemiological research, pharmaceutical research, and the development of laboratory screening tests, which can provide early diagnosis of the onset of physical disease. The search for cures to all of mankind's diseases not just a dream; rather, it is a concerted effort among health scientists and medical doctors, worldwide. Of course what man seeks is not simply a disease-free physical body; man also seeks freedom from the symptoms of stress arising from the competitive pressures of living in modern society.

Quantum mechanical science has proved to us that the human organism is not just a physical structure made of molecules; but, like everything else, is ultimately composed of energetic particles, occupying discrete energy levels, in space-time. We are constantly changing, fading, and flowing, just like the sea.

Modern science; is steadily making progress in the development of devices to both measure *and induce* subtle changes in bodily energy flows. As an example, the *Infratonic QGM* device (US-FDA-approved for the relief of muscular pain) was developed out of scientific research conducted in Beijing China, which investigated the physical characteristics of laying-on-of-hands healers.

It was discovered that most *Chigong healers* were able to emit an *infrasonic* (inaudible, low frequency) sound from their hands, 100 times greater in amplitude than those emitted from the hands of average individuals. Experiments conducted in hospitals and research laboratories found that infrasonic sound was, indeed, effective in increasing vitality, accelerating healing, and strengthening the immune function of test subjects.

In addition, professional schools of energy healing have recently emerged on the healthcare scene: the Barbara Ann Brennan School of Healing, a laying-on-of-hands healing institute, with a four-year program that attracts students from all areas of medical science; and, the Caroline Myss Program, a four-year medical intuition program, which includes an internship affiliation with a Doctor of Medicine, or Doctor of Osteopathy.

To bridge current and emergent energy-related disciplines, in medical science and medical practice, the International Society for the Study of Subtle Energies and Energy Medicine (ISSSEEM) has held annual conferences since 1990. The ISSSEEM brings together world-renowned scholars, practitioners, and speakers to share theoretical and applied subtle-energy research; e.g., Larry Dossey, M.D, Elliott Dacher, M.D, and Robert O. Becker, M.D.

Today, more than 100,000 health professionals, worldwide, practice energy healing as a therapeutic modality. The University Of Arizona School Of Medicine is now introducing energy healing as one of its teaching tools, thanks to the work of Dr. Andrew Weil. Universities around the world are incorporating energy healing in programs of medical and behavioral study. On the basis of these realities, it is difficult to deny the efficacy of energy healing.

In Poland and Russia, energy healers are licensed by their governments. Hopefully, such licensing soon will be required in the United States. Far beyond regulating energy healing through the laying-on of hands, licensure would grant to dedicated, skillful, and highly educated healers the professional acknowledgment and respect, so long overdue.

This work has explored the influence of the mind and soul on the human body, the existence and function of the chakras system, the existence of the human energy field, and the effectiveness of laying-on-of-hands energy therapy. We have learned that the human body is itself, an energetic system, which is affected by the flow of life-force energy in a dynamic way. Our emotions and life experiences, even physical traumas, are stored in our energy body; negative cellular memories, can create blockages to vital energy flow.

It is clear from the research presented in this book that, by keeping the life force in a state of balance, all systems of the body remain in balance. Conversely, if the flow of life force is blocked — or heavily accumulated — physical, mental, or emotional illness may occur.

The laying-on of hands as an energy-healing therapy; is a gentle, non-invasive, and highly effective way to release vital energy blockage and, thereby, promote energy flow. The human body manifests the most obvious symptoms of physical disease; however, all levels of the energy body reflect the flow of life force within: A skillful energy healer can effectively treat illness stored in the human energy field (HEF), even before its manifestation in the physical body.

An energy healer is someone who is trained both to perceive the aura and to channel universal energy to the client's HEF, for the purpose of facilitating beneficial changes. The healer must be attuned to universal life energy to be able to accomplish this transfer. The universal energy field is composed of many different frequencies, or rays of varying intensity. A primary goal of the healer is to achieve attunement to higher frequencies of universal life energy, with higher-order energy rays.

It is only through on-going education, meditation and higher consciousness development that the prospective healer will reach his (or her) ultimate potential. Constant practice in focusing and directing the flow of healing energy is essential to the successful treatment of illness; like in anything else in life, practice makes perfect.

Using universal life-force energy, as part of the healing process, enhances the body's own biological ability to heal itself. All healing is basically self-healing: a physician can set two bone fragments in place, but the body, itself, finally heals the split. The physician simply directs and facilitates the process. The prescribed medications will provide the body with the necessary substances to fight an infection, but it is the body's own wisdom that will destroy harmful bacteria.

The energy healer acts as a channel to ultimately supply the physical body with the needed universal life force, which ignites its own, self-healing capabilities: that is why each of us is a healer. I do not mean to deny that there are gifted healers; however, it is clear that energy healing is a skill that can be learned by any compassionate human being who decides to dedicate his (or her) life to easing the pains of humanity.

Energy healing is a means of facilitating physical, mental, emotional and spiritual; healing processes. The energy-healing practitioner re-aligns vital energy flow, thereby re-activating the mind/body/spirit connection to eliminate blockages to self-healing. Energy healing should never be considered as a complete therapy alone. It is designed to complement traditional medical therapy and not to replace it. Therefore, the healer should not receive a client that refuses to be treated in conjunction with a medical doctor. Moreover, the healer should not, unless he (or she) is also a medical doctor, attempt to diagnose disease or medicate the client. To diagnose disease and to prescribe drugs therefore are privileges reserved for those who have attended a recognized school of medicine, to attain the training and knowledge requisite to maintain human health.

FINAL THOUGHTS ON ENERGY HEALING

The connection between mind, body, and spirit is difficult to prove scientifically; however, conventional health practitioners are increasingly coming to recognize that a holistic approach to healthcare is both effective and affordable.

Rethinking the mechanisms of health and disease is not an easy task; however, the paradigm shift required of mid-nineteenth-century physicians was no easier: As William Loeliger, M.D., wisely reminded us in one of his speeches:

"In the mid-1800s physicians encountered the thoroughly radical idea of hand washing. A Viennese physician by the name of Semmelweis proposed that childbirth fever could be reduced by having the obstetricians wash their hands before delivery. Obstetricians called the idea preposterous. Of course, at that time, there was no germ theory of disease and no one had ever seen a bacterium. Even after a dramatic reduction in mortality was convincingly demonstrated by a controlled study, skeptical physicians could not accept the fact that there was some invisible factor causing disease that they were helping to spread. Semmelweis was labeled a troublemaker and run out of town. The concept of energy healing is in a similar situation now. Without a coherent theory of how it works that fits into our current model, physicians are very reluctant to recognize its value."

Fortunately, opposition to energy healing is beginning to lessen. At the request of their clients, plastic surgeons (and others) are inviting energy healers to their surgeries. Many have reported that those clients, assisted by an energy healer, presented less bleeding, faster anesthesia recovery, less need for pain medication, and shorter hospital stays.

My purpose in having this work published is twofold: First, the need for continuing self-improvement and education needs be stressed to energy healers. Energy healing work, like any other field of endeavor, is in a state of flux. To better serve their fellow man, it is imperative that healers keep themselves updated and open-minded; actively developing a state of higher consciousness. Second, this writing constitutes an outreach to medical professionals, an appeal for synergy: physicians and energy healers partnering for the benefit of human health. Collaboration between these latter professionals is a win-win situation for both doctor and client.

With the sheer volume of today's caseloads, Medical Doctors can no longer give each of their clients the love, empathy, and individualized attention that the energy healer is bound to give. The world of today is saturated with psychosomatic illness, with people who have nowhere to turn; they visit their physicians for peace of mind, perhaps, more frequently than for relief of physical suffering.

Healers, however, recognize that the origin of most disease is psychosomatic, i.e., caused by unrest of the mind: frustrations, sickness of the soul, and emotional disturbances. Because disturbances of the psyche cannot be immediately remedied by physical medicine, they can be a source of frustration to the healthcare professional. Curiously, afflictions of the mind and spirit are amenable to energy healing: they exist, fundamentally, in the HEF. With appropriate energy therapy, with compassionate understanding, vital energy flow is re-aligned; re-activating the mind/body/spirit connection to eliminate blockages to self-healing.

I look forward to the day when physicians and energy healers collaborate together. While their therapies are separate, the one based upon physical anatomy and the other upon energy anatomy, they are complementary approaches to healing. It is common sense that, where both healing disciplines are beneficial, the client should be entitled to both.

85

In closing, I leave the prospective energy healer with the following caution: Be open and learn to deal well with skepticism. It is just temporary! Perform your healing work to the best of your ability, no matter what others say or do, because to borrow "Mother Theresa's words on fulfilling one's mission" at the end it will not be between you and them anyway, but between you and God."

I hope the first part of this book was helpful to further your knowledge in "how" energy healing works. In the next part of this book we will explore the science and the healing capabilities of Aromatherapy. Please come along to the miracle path of fragrant healing.

PART II

WHAT IS AROMATHERAPY?

The word aromatherapy means "treatment using scents". Aromatherapy is the use and application of essential oils, through different methods, to enhance the well-being of the body, mind and spirit. It is the art, and science, of using oils extracted from aromatic plants to enhance health and beauty. Aromatherapy has been around and has been practiced in one form or another since the beginning of civilization.

With origins dating back 5,000 years, Aromatherapy is truly one of the oldest methods of holistic healing. In the beginning the ancient man was dependent on his surroundings for everything from food, to shelter and clothing. Being so eagerly aware of everything around him, and how it could be used for survival, he quickly discovered methods to preserve food and treat ailments through herbs and aromatics.

Ancient Egyptians used infusion to extract the oils from aromatic plants which were used for medicinal and cosmetic purposes. Accordance to Shen Nong's herbal book, (dating back to approximately 2700 BC), ancient Chinese civilizations also used some form of aromatics from over 300 plants.

Ayurveda, the traditional medical system of India, has been practiced for more than 3,000. Ayurveda practitioners use dried and fresh herbs, as well as aromatic massage as important aspects of their therapies. Likewise many other ancient cultures writing confirms that the use of herbs and flowers in their therapies.

Egyptian hieroglyphics dating more than 5,000 years is an evidence of the ancient use of aromatics vapor inhaled in the air. Hippocrates, the famous Greek Physician, whose works were published around 400 B.C. recognized that burning certain aromatic substances offered protection against contagious diseases. In Roman as well as Greek bath houses, aromatic oils were extensively used, as prescribed by Hippocrates, for health, because of the antibacterial and antiviral properties of particular aromatic oils. He said: "the way to health is to have an aromatic bath and scented massage every day".

The holy anointing oil that God directed Moses to make was a synergy blend of myrrh, sweet cinnamon, calamus, cassia, and olive oil. This synergy would have been a powerful antiviral and antibiotic substance. Cinnamon is a powerful antiviral and antibacterial and antifungal agent. Myrrh is an effective antiseptic. It stimulates cellular growth and has healing effects on open wounds, ulcers, and boils.

Aromas were part of Jesus life from beginning to end. At Jesus' birth, the kings brought gifts of gold, frankincense, and myrrh - gold, perhaps, to help financially, frankincense and myrrh as incense material and medicine. Myrrh is wonderful healing oil and one of the most versatile. It is antiseptic, supports the immune system, enhances the body's natural defenses and is great for oxygenating to body tissues and mood elevating. Frankincense is anti-inflammatory, antiseptic, astringent, antidepressant and cicatrizant to name a few. Two days before the Crucifixion, Mary Magdalene took "a pound of ointment of spikenard, very costly and anointed the feet of Jesus, and wiped his feet with her hair, and the house was filled with the odor of the ointment" (John 12:3—7). Spikenard's effect is extremely sedative; obviously she knew Jesus was going to need it.

Ancient people seemed to intuitively know that the properties of the essential oils of flowers and plants were all they needed to reap physical, emotional, mental and spiritual benefits. They regularly used aromatics oils for practically everything from physical healing and emotional cleansing to enhancement of prayer and meditation and purification.

Aromatherapy and spirituality merge as one in many of the spiritual traditions of the world. The long aromatic tradition is often hidden in symbols which origins we have long since ceased to question or remember. For example, the word "rosary", comes from the fact that early Christian priests wore garlands of roses around their necks on feast days. The first rosaries were made from 165 rosebuds. And the menorah, the famous Jewish candlestick with seven arms, which is the emblem of Israel for over three thousand years, is a material replica of the fragrant healing plants of the *Salvia* species that not long ago covered the Mount Moriah in Jerusalem.

Aromatherapy has been used widely by several cultures for religious purpose and to enhance spirituality. Every evening in India, the air is rich with the aroma of incense burning at home shrines. In Ethiopian Coptic and Orthodox Christian churches the air is filled with the smoke fragrant with the aroma of the smoldering resins, frankincense and myrrh. Muslims use lavish quantities of sweet-smelling rose water to provide fragrance to mosques and other holy places. The Native Americans use the fragrant herbs of sage, cedar, and sweetgrass which are put on the hot rocks to release their aroma molecules into the humid atmosphere. Tibetans go up on the roofs of their houses, each dawn, to light stoves in which they burn bundles of juniper with the intention to force the sky door open. As the smoke rises from the houses and fragrance fills the air, prayers can be heard. At Chinese Buddhist shrines, clouds of fragrant smoke rise from handfuls of incense sticks.

The word messiah means "the anointed one" Kings had from very early times been anointed as a sign of their kingship, and Jesus was a king in the line of David. Shakespeare described the spiritual and irreversible nature of the anointing of Richard II: "Not all the water in the rough rude sea: Can wash the balm from an anointed king; the breath of worldly men cannot depose: The deputy elected of the Lord."

The first English king to be anointed was Egforth of Mercia, in

1785. The anointment ceremony was derived from the Jewish traditional described in the Old Testament. The royal anointing oil ingredients' have changed little over hundreds of years. Although the coronation oil has traditionally been prepared by the royal physicians, it has been always applied in a spiritual context. At the coronation of Queen Elizabeth II in June 1953 it was composed of the essential oils of neroli, rose, cinnamon and jasmine, benzoin, musk, civet, and ambergris, in a base of sesame oil. The only difference between this blend and the blend used in the coronation of Charles I in A.D 1626 was the replacement of the "oil of being" by sesame oil.

Aromatherapy is already slowly getting into the mainstream. Many of today's alternative medicine providers already incorporated aromatherapy into their practices. Many naturopaths, massage therapists, chiropractors, sports medicine therapists, psychotherapists, aestheticians, Ayurvedic practitioners, and practitioners of Chinese Medicine incorporate the use of essential oils into their healing art to enhance desired effects. In Japan, engineers are incorporating aroma systems into new buildings. In one such application, the fragrance from lemon and eucalyptus are used in the bank teller counters to keep the staff alert, while the scent of lavender and rosemary is pumped into the customer area to calm down the waiting customers.

There is no doubt that the high frequency of essential oils can enhance any alternative method of healing, working in all levels: mind, body and spirit. Aroma reaches and influences the deepest human instincts, feelings and thoughts.

Nonetheless, it's recently popularity; aromatherapy is still a field that scientists are just beginning to explore more broadly. It is very encouraging to know that researchers have found that we respond to aromatherapy within one to three seconds after inhalation or physical touch of the oil, fast response, not yet met by any other form or substance.

Fragrance has been said to alert the gods to our presence. Personally, I prefer to think that fragrance is a tool to alert us to god's presence and acts as a tool to help the human mind to be focused and receptive to spiritual guidance.

ESSENTIAL OILS
PRECIOUS HEALING AGENT OF ALL TIMES

Many writings tell us that the distillation of aromatic plants was used over 5000 years ago. Some say that aromatherapy began in China, some say India. According to a papyrus found in the Temple of Edfu, dating back to 4500 BC, the Egyptians were using fragrant oils for rituals, ceremony and medicine. Three oils used in the embalming process were cedarwood, myrrh and frankincense. Well-preserved oils were found in alabaster jars in King Tut's tomb. When did the use of essential oils really start? If we refer to the beginning of the history of creation we will realize that the beginning of genesis tell us what might be as well the beginning of the use of essential oils, "God placed the first man and woman in a garden where they would live and continuously breathe the oils of plants floating in the atmosphere." (Genesis 2 BSB (biblehub.com)

According to the Bible, the three Wise Men brought the oils of frankincense and myrrh to the Christ child. In those days, frankincense was considered more precious than gold, both for its ability to heal and protect as well as to enhance prayer and meditation. Myrrh is an effective antiseptic and on stimulates cellular growth. Its healing effects on open wounds, ulcers, and boils were famous even before Biblical times. There are 188 references to oils in the Bible, and some, such as frankincense, myrrh, rosemary, hyssop and spikenard, were used for the anointing and healing of the sick.

As late as in the nineteenth century, medical practitioners still carried a little bag filled with aromatics on top of their walking sticks, so they could inhale them when visiting any contagious cases and protect themselves from contamination.

The holy anointing oil that God directed Moses to make from myrrh, sweet cinnamon, calamus, cassia, and olive oil, would have been a powerful antiviral and antibiotic substance, the use of which gave protection and treatment to all those to whom it was administered. Cinnamon is a powerful antiviral and antibacterial agent as well as being antifungal.

Essential oils are the subtle, aromatic and volatile life-force which are extracted from certain species of flowers, grasses, fruits, seed, bark, leaves, roots, and trees. The oil is concentrated in different parts of the plant. Geranium oil comes from the leaves and stalks, Vetiver oil is made from the chopped roots of the grass species, Mandarin, lemon, lime, grapefruit, and bergamot oils are squeezed from the peel of the fruits, Myrrh, frankincense, and benzoin oils are extracted from the resin of their respective trees, ginger oil comes from the root-like stems which grow under or along the ground, pine oil is extracted from the needles and twigs, Cinnamon oil is extracted from the bark of the tree.

Essential oils are extracted from the plant by a variety of means, depending again on the particular species. The most desirable method is steam distillation, although other important methods are solvent extraction, expression, effleurage, and maceration. Steam distillation is a process known to have been used by Babylonias, Chinese, East Indians, Egyptians and Sumerians at least as far back as 3500 B.C.

In order to produce the purest of oils, it may be very costly and require several hundred or thousands of pounds of plants to extract one pound of oil. About sixty thousand rose blossoms are required to produce one ounce of rose oil, whereas in the lavender plant the essential oil is more abundant and approximately 230 pounds will yield 1 pound of oil. The Sandalwood tree must be thirty years old, thirty feet high, before it is cut down for distillation. Taking it in consideration it is easy to understand why the price of some essential oils is so high. For example: if you consider that takes eight million jasmine blossoms, that must be picked by hand before the sun becomes hot on the very first day they open, to produce 2.2 pounds of oil, you can understand why that is one of the most expensive oils on the market.

Therapeutic grade essential oils can be highly penetrating which greatly enhances their ability to be effective. It is theoretical assumed that substances with low molecular weight will have the capability to penetrate the skin. The essentials oils constituents are mostly below 1000 m (m = molecular weight), what led us to assume that when essentials oils are applied on the skin; they will travel and reach the bloodstream.

Many bacteria are anaerobic, meaning that they can only survive in the absence of oxygen. Cancer cells increases in the absence of oxygen. When many kinds of microbes and cancer cells are exposed to oxygen, they die. Oxygen is a very powerful antioxidant. Therapeutic grade essential oils proved to increase oxygen to the body at a rate of 21% while herbs and vitamins give us only about a 6 -7 % increase in oxygen. Mineral compounds and hydrogen peroxide provide a 9% increase.

The three primary elements in both humans and essential oils are oxygen, carbon and hydrogen. Taking this fact in consideration, there is no doubt that the equal chemistry is what makes essential oils one of the most compatible of all substances with human biochemistry. Comparing even further the similarity of the Protein-like structures of the essential oils compared and those in the human cells and tissues, we will understand even more why essential oils are readily identified and accepted by the body.

The Natural Medicine Alert, published by the Young Life Research Clinic (YLRC) and Institute of Natural Medicine, February/March 2001 issue, published an article entitled: "Fruits and Premature Aging". The article backed up by 80 references stated that most free radicals contain electrically unbalanced oxygen atoms. Free radical molecules frantically look for missing electron and can aggressively attack our tissues and cells causing unhealthy mutations and irreversible damage. It will suppress our immune system and can also affect us by accelerated aging and a host of other maladies. If we continuously receive vaccinations and long term, or excess medications, it can even damage the DNA of our cells permanently.

How do we fight the free radicals? The more foods and substances rich in anti-oxidants that absorb free radicals we include in our diet, more we reduce the free radical activity and the more youthful and disease-free we will remain.

Scientists at Tufts University have developed a scale for the U.S. Department of Agriculture called the ORAC test (Oxygen Radical Absorption Capacity). The ORAC test determines how capable a particular food is in destroying free radicals. The essentials oils tested proved to be extremely high in antioxidants, with essential oil of clove tested far higher than any food, making it an extremely potent antioxidant.

FOOD ORAC SCORES (based on a 3.5 oz (100 ml) sample)

Food	ORAC Score
Strawberries	1,540
Raspberries	1,220
Beets	840
Blueberries	2,400
Oranges	750
Carrots	210

Essential oils have the highest ORAC scores of any known substance!

ESSENTIAL OILS/ BOTANICAL NAME	ORAC SCORE
Sandalwood (Santalum Album)	1,655
Roman Chamomile (Chamaemelum nobile)	2,446
Juniper (Juniperus osteosperma)	2,517
Rosemary (Rosmarinus officinalis)	3,309
Lavender (Lavendula angustifolia)	3,669
Spearmint (Mentha spicata)	5,398
Helichrysum (Helichrysum italicum)	17,420
Lemongrass (Cymbopogen flexuosus)	17,765
Orange (Citrus aurantium)	18,898
Eucalyptus Eucalyptus (Eucalyptus (Eucalyptus globulus)	24,157
Rose of Sharon (Cistus ladanifer)	38,648
Cinnamon Bark (Cinnamamum verum)	103,448
Mountain Savory (*Satureja montana*)	113,071
Oregano (*Origanum compactum*)	153,007
Thyme (*Thymus vulgaris*)	159,590
Clove (*Syzigium aromaticum*)	10,786,875

References:

The ORAC test developed by scientists at Tufts University for the U.S. Department of Agriculture.

Considering the numbers above, two drops of essential oil of clove have the anti-oxidant power of 5 lb of carrots, 2.5 quarts of carrot juice, 10 oranges, 20 ounces or orange juice, 2.5 pounds of beets, 1 pint of beet juice, 4 cups of raspberries or 2.5 cups of blueberries. It is easy to figure out the value to include a drop of clove essential oil in your daily nutritional program.

Presently, we can count on the help of approximately three hundred of essential oils, which constitute an extremely effective medicinal system.

Many of these are the active ingredient in drugs prescribed by the orthodox Western system of medicine, or they are the inspiration for chemical copies.

For effective therapeutic use it is crucial that only therapeutic grade essential oils be used, which means, only natural plant essences which have been extracted by steam distillation, solvent extraction, expression or maceration. It is quite pointless buying any other product, no matter how alluring its aroma may be, because reconstituted products or chemical copies of natural essences simply do not work for medicinal purposes for a very simple reason, it has no "life force."

Adulteration of essential oils is becoming more and more common these days. As the demand for them grows, the supply of top-grade essential oils diminishes. With the scarcity comes the temptation to thin the oils with solvents, and then add synthetic fragrance. In the last several years, France exported 100 times more lavender oil than it produced. This can only be possible if the oil is being thinned. Thinned oils may be labeled as pure essential oils, but there is no life force in an adulterated essential oil.

True lavender oil *(Lavandula angustifolia)* is expensive and difficult to find. Most of the lavender oil sold in America today is actually the hybrid, Lavandin, grown and distilled in China, Russia, France and Tasmania. It is shipped to France and cut with synthetic linolyl acetate to improve the fragrance. Then propylene glycol, DEP or DOP (odorless solvents) are added and it is labeled as *Lavandula officinalis.* Many times it also goes through heat processing to burn off the camphor the hybrid contains and then thinned with more linolyl acetate to appear as lavender. These bottles line the shelves of health food stores, herb shops and department stores, selling for $5.00 to $7.00 per half ounce. Unfortunately, most consumers don't know the difference.

Another essential oil frequently adulterated is Frankincense. This essential oil requires 12 hours of steam distillation from expensive resin to be therapeutic-grade. Inexpensive frankincense oil that sells for $25 an ounce or less is invariably distilled with alcohol or other solvents. Lemon oil is another favorite for adulteration. Terpene waste fractions left over from the industrial refining of citrus products and/or synthetic limonene is often purchased from chemical houses and used to dilute or "extend" genuine lemon oil. Since terpenes and limonene naturally occur in lemon oil, even a gas chromatograph cannot distinguish between synthetic and natural limonene.

The petrochemical solvents in adulterated oils can cause intense allergic reactions and toxic accumulations; they can cause rashes, burning, and skin irritations. It is very important to know about the integrity of the company from whom you are buying the essential oil. It is also very important for the company or vendor to know about the integrity of the oil.

ESSENTIAL OILS CHEMISTRY

It is not the intention of this book, to provide you with a lesson in organic chemistry, but to be able to use essential oils, safely, in a meaningful, caring and effective way, not at random, or indiscriminately one needs to have at least a basic understanding of the chemistry of the essential oils before responsibly using them. A little knowledge of oils' chemistry will come in handy when you are ready to blend your own essential oils' synergy.

Chemists have identified more than 3,000 different aromatic molecules, and new ones are continually being discovered. The list of the physiological and pharmacological properties of aromatic molecules includes almost all the organs and all the functions of the organism, from skin conditions to psychological disturbances. The list of the physiological and pharmacological properties of aromatic molecules includes almost all the organs and all the functions of the organism, from skin conditions to psychological disturbances.

Scientists are continuously studying the interaction of the plant chemicals within the human body. Until more is discovered, the knowledge of the basic composition of each oil, contribute to the overall background knowledge of aromatherapy, thus promoting confidence and aiding in the selection of the oils to be used.

ESSENTIAL OIL'S CHEMICAL MAKEUP

The various chemical components of each essential oil combine in different ways to create specific oils. Some oils have hundreds components, others have a few. Those hundreds of chemical constituents work in synergy to produce various effects on the body. This can explain the different pharmacologic or therapeutic properties of a single essential oil. For example, Lavender can be expectorant, bactericidal, antifungal, antiseptic, analgesic and anti-depressant. The single oil properties also can be changed and or increased by blending two or more oils together. Therefore, the application of essential oils is endless.

Alcohols

Alcohols are bactericidal (kill bacteria), energizing, vitalizing, anti-viral and diuretic, toning, they create an uplifting quality and are regarded as non-toxic, and non-irritating. The pancreas produces 32 kinds of alcohol for use in human metabolism. Some of the most beneficial molecules in essential oils are alcohols. Linalol and terpineol are two common terpene alcohols which are both germicidal and non-toxic. Alcohols are not water soluble and evaporate quite slowly. Because they are less prone to oxidation they will keep much longer. Essential oils which are high in alcohols include rose, petitgrain, rosewood, peppermint, myrtle, tea tree, sandalwood, patchouli and ginger.

Phenols

This chemical group contains some of the most stimulating, bactericidal, and immune boosting essential oils. They are immune stimulants, invigorating, warming, potential skin irritants and can produce slight liver toxicity if taken in high doses for extended periods of time. Phenols are responsible for the fragrance of oil. Phenols are water soluble and evaporate more quickly than oils that do not contain phenols. Pharmaceutically, phenol is used in lip balms and cough drops. Phenols create condition where viruses and bacteria cannot live. They contain high levels of oxygenating molecules and have antioxidant properties. Also they clear the receptor sites on the cells, promoting clear communications between cells and avoiding body's malfunctions. Its capacity of clearing the cells' site, indicate that oils high in phenol are excellent for use in energy healing during the cell's clearing process. Examples of oils that have high content of phenol include clove (90%,) cinnamon leaf (86.0%), oregano (75%), savory (40%), Fennel Sweet (62%)

Monoterpenes

Monoterpenes are very stimulating, anti-septic, and analgesic, and have anti-viral properties. These oils are usually quite strong and may cause skin irritation. Monoterpenes make up the hydrocarbon group. Monoterpenes are some of the smallest molecules in aromatherapy, very quick to come to the nose, and very quick to evaporate. The majority of the lemon scented oils fall into the high monoterpene category. (Lemon (87%), Orange (90%), Eucalyptus Dives, (30%), Grapefruit (96%) Others oils also high in monoterpene are Galbanum (80%), Angelica (73%), Hyssop ((70%), Peppermint (45%), Juniper (42%), Frankincense (40%), Spruce (38%), Pine (30%). Besides it's variety of healing properties, another important ability of the monoterpenes is that they can reprogram miswritten information in the cellular memory, which makes oils high in monoterpenes ideal for use in energy working while clearing old ideas or emotional patterns.

Sesquiterpenes

Sesquiterpenes are some of the longest carbon chains found in the essential oils, fifteen carbons and twenty-four hydrogens per molecule—molecular weight 204 amu) Oils high in sesquiterpenes are very thick and tenacious, long lasting in their smell. Properties include anti-phlogistic (moves fluids), anti-inflammatory, sedative, anti-viral, potentially anti-carcinogenic, bacteriostatic and immune stimulant. Research has shown that sesquiterpenes have the ability to surpass the blood-brain barrier and enter the brain tissue. Sesquiterpenes outstanding anti-inflammatory properties have been under serious study recently. Studies on sesquiterpenes to treat cancer, reveals that they can also erase or deprogram miswritten codes in the DNA. Again, a possibility that we cannot disregard in using essentials oils for energy work purpose. Deprograming miswritten codes in the DNA might be all that it takes for an effective cellular blockage clearing. Oils high in sesquiterpenes are: Cedarwood (50%), Vetiver (97%), Spikenard (93%), Sandalwood (Aloes) 90%, Black Pepper (30%), Patchouli (50%), Myrrh (39%), Yarrow (45%) Ginger, (55%) and Ylang Ylang (40%).

Esters

Esters are chemically the most neutral of the essential oil component. Esters are the compounds resulting from the reaction of an alcohol with an acid (known as esterification). Esters are very common and are found in a large number of essential oils. They are anti-fungal, sedative, calming, spasmolytic, fungicidal and anti-inflammatory. Essential oils containing high amounts of esters include Roman chamomile (75%), lavender (45%), clary sage (70%), bergamot (40%), Petitgrain (55%) and Jasmin (54%)

Lactones

Lactones are an ester group which also has a carbon ring attached; they are some of the most anti-inflammatory compounds known. Lactones can be found in several essential oils, such as Yarrow, Tarragon, sage and orange to name a few.

Ethers

Ethers (sometimes called phenylpropane ethers), are very harmonizing to the nervous system. They are antiseptic, stimulant, expectorant (increase secretions), spasmolytic and diuretic. This group includes such oils as clove (90%), basil (25%), tarragon (70%), thyme (40%) and fennel (62%). They are characterized by their very sweet fragrance.

All therapeutic essential oils have some anti-bacterial properties. They increase the production of white blood cells, which help fight infectious illnesses. Research has found that people who use therapeutics essential oils on regular base, have a higher level of resistance to illnesses, colds, flues, and diseases than the average person. And when those people contract a cold, flu, or other illness, will recover 60-70 percent faster than those who do not use essential oils.

Essential Oil chemistry is such a fascinating area for exploration. For the readers that are interested to further develop their knowledge on therapeutic grade essential oil, I highly recommend Dr. David Stewart book "The Chemistry of Essential Oils made simple". I was blessed with the opportunity to take classes with Dr. Stewart. His knowledge and chemistry passion was incomparable.

ESSENTIAL OIL'S FREQUENCY

Just by observing the chemical makeup of the essential oils it is obvious their outstanding capability to help the human body to heal, but there is also another very important factor to consider. It is the matter of frequency!

In his book, The Body Electric, Dr. Robert O. Becker, established that the human body has an electrical frequency and that much about a person's health can be determined by its frequency. Frequency is the measurable rate of electrical energy flow that is constant between any two points and is measured in hertz (Hz).

Tanio's Calibrated Frequency Monitor (CFM) also has been used to measure the frequencies of essential oils and their effect on human frequencies when applied to the body. The table below shows the findings.

Essential Oil	Frequency
Rose *(Rosa damascena)*	320 MHz
Helichrysum *(Helichrysum ltalicum)*	181 MHz
Ravensara *(Ravensara aromatica)*	181 MHz
Lavender *(Lavendula angustifolia)*	118 MHz
Blue Tansy *(Tanacetum annum)*	105 MHz.
German Chamomile *(Matricaria recutita)*	105 MHz
Melissa *(Melissa officinalis)*	102 MHz
Juniper *(Juniperus osteosperma)*	98 MHz
Angelica (Angelica archangelica)	85 MHz
Peppermint (Mentha peperita)	78 MHz
Galbanum (Ferula Gummosa)	56 MHz
Basil (Ocimum basilicum)	52 MHz

In the 1920s a scientist-inventor named Royal Raymond Rife invented a new kind of microscope. He stated that every disease has a frequency. He found that certain frequencies prevent and even destroy the development of disease. He suggested that substances with a higher frequency would destroy diseases of a lower frequency.

Dr. Valnet an M.D. from France, who is a medical researcher and essential oil expert, says about clove oil, "it has been found to have electronic constituents which are opposed to cancer and viral diseases."

The frequency factor in cure of diseases appears to be of utmost importance. The essential oils high frequency showed in the table above encourage its use to maintain our health free of disease.

So far we have been reviewing how essential interact with our physical body, and how useful they are in aiding us in the prevention and in some cases cure of illness, but how does essential oil help us at the emotional level?

THE OLFACTORY TRACT

The New Atlas of Human Anatomy (1999 Barnes & Noble's book) describes the olfactory tract and its connection to the limbic system as follows:

"Olfactory tracts within the bulbs lead to the olfactory cortex on the lateral and medial surfaces of the temporal lobe of the brain. This primitive region of the cortex, which forms part of the limbic, is the primary olfactory area, where the conscious awareness of smells occurs. Some smell information from the nose travels to other parts of the limbic system and also to the hypothalamus, provoking subconscious emotional and memory-linked responses to smells, for example, the odor of a particular food evoking memories of childhood."

A number of brain components — known collectively as the limbic system—encircle the brain stem close to the inner border of the cerebrum. These components include the hippocampus, the amygdala, the hypothalamus, and part of the thalamus and the fornix, which links these parts together. The limbic system is the emotional brain, which deals with basic emotions such as fear, pain, pleasure, anger, sorrow, sexual excitement, and affection. It interacts closely with the cerebral cortex to produce a close relationship between feelings and thoughts; this interaction provides a conscious awareness of emotions and also enables us to control and limit the effects of basic and primitive emotional responses, and not express them under inappropriate circumstances. The hippocampus and amygdala also play a part in memory by converting new information into long-term memories.

Essential oils connect directly into the hippocampus and amygdala areas of the limbic system. The only way to stimulate this gland is with fragrance, or the sense of smell. This is why essential oils may play a major role in our effort to release emotional trauma, and may profoundly affect our mood and emotion. Essential oils are highly aromatic and, therefore, many of the benefits can be obtained by simply inhaling them. This can be done by breathing in the fragrance from the bottle, or they can be diffused into the room. There are many other ways to use essential oils in your daily life. We will review some of them in the next chapter. Essential oils stimulate in the human body the secretion of antibodies, neurotransmitters, endorphins, hormones, and enzymes. They are as alive as human beings are both chemically and electrically.

For the last 40 years essential oils have been researched and used therapeutically in Germany, Switzerland, France and England. Aromatherapy is taught in medical schools in France and England and the oils are used by doctors in many European Hospitals.

ESSENTIAL OILS & EMOTIONAL RELEASE

Considering the olfactory tract and its connection with the limbic system, it's easy to understand that scent stimulation of the amygdala is the key to unlocking and releasing stored trauma in the body. Our feelings and emotions are not necessary negative or positive. It is only when we suppress feelings and emotions that are too overwhelming for our body to deal with, that we create blockages and imbalance in our energy field.

Today's science has abundant studies results, proving that our emotional & mental states rule our physical body. In other words, emotions & feelings are not in our mind, they are in our body. Therefore, the true healing must start at the source; in other words, at the mental & emotional levels.

Clearing an energy blockage requires identifying the underlying emotions, understanding the pattern, and, especially, learning the lesson; so as to avoid the repetition of the same pattern. Until we learn from an experience, we continue to recreate similar situations. Similar situations from the past will often resurface; many can be released simply by acknowledging them, others will require much more work.

In my Energy healing practice I have had several encounters with those "hard to release" emotional patterns. Being fascinated by aromatherapy since my childhood, and knowing how much our emotions are connected with our sense of smell, I decided to experiment with essential oils as a tool to facilitate the release of those emotional patterns.

My goal was to alter the client state of consciousness during an energy work, using the high frequency of the essentials oils to open the subconscious doors and disengage the barriers that stop us from releasing our traumas. The oils oxygenate the cells and bring its blockages to the surface, ready to be released.

Essential Oil molecules are the smallest molecules of all matter. (Less than 500 atomic mass units). They have the ability to penetrate the so called "Blood-Brain Barrier." When you inhale oil molecules into the back passages of your nose, they go straight to the brain in a central part called the amygdala or diencephalon, in other words: the headquarters of the limbic system.

This system is the area of your brain that manages the storage and filing system for all your emotional experiences, much like in the same way the file manager in your computer manages your computer's files. When we have an emotional experience, especially a traumatic or painful one, the amygdala assigns a part of your body to remember that experience until you are ready to deal with it. Much like in the same way, that when we get our tax return in the mail, we file it to avoid having to deal with it right way. So, what happens if we keep our tax return filed and do not deal with it? We will get another notice in the mail, more expensive and more painful. In the same way, emotions that are not dealt with, keep repeating in our life, more and more painfully, until we become brave and learn to deal with them once and for all.

Although we might not be very selective deciding where we are going to file our Tax Return, (we just want to be rid of it) the amygdala has a very efficient filing system. Because each organ of the human body has a specific vibrational frequency, and so does each emotion. The amygdala sends the emotion to be filed to a place in our body that matches the exact vibrational frequency of that specific emotion. That is why we carry anger blockages in the liver, stress blockages in the stomach, and fear blockages in the kidneys and so on. Those emotions that are not dealt with, sooner or later, will resurface, to give us another opportunity to learn from it. Furthermore, the blockages stored in our organs, glands and systems, lower our physical vibrational frequency. When our physical vibrational frequency drops below a certain point, disease may occur. What happens if we raise our body frequency during energy work? The emotional blockage will disengage and come out to become amenable to healing.

Dr. Rachel Sarah Herz, the Assistant Professor of Psychology at Brown University, researches the connection between the sense of smell and memory. She believes that the only way to stimulate the amygdala is with fragrance, or the sense of smell. The olfactory nerve synapses are routed almost directly into the amygdala, in the limbic system, which is associated with memory and emotion. She stated that her studies led her to believe that emotions are so linked to smell, that probably, if we did not have the sense of smell we would not have emotions. Probably that is why the smell of baking cookies brings back memories of our grandmother's kitchen, or a lover's fragrance takes us back to the past.

Therapeutic essential oils carry electrical charges, usually electrons or negatives ions, which are healing and healthful. Essential oils are also energetic. They generate nanovolts of electricity (billionths of a volt) at megahertz frequencies (that's in the radio frequency range of millions of cycles per second.)

We know essential oil characteristics, thanks to Tainio Technology, an independent division of Eastern State University in Cheny, Washington. Tainio has developed the first frequency monitor and had has done experiments measuring the frequency of different substances. Tainio's experiment measured the frequency of several essential oils, and the result was just astonishing. For example: Rose oil has a frequency of 320 Mhz. (The highest of all known substances).

Tainio's work has also determined that the average frequency of the human body during the daytime is 62-68 Mhz. (A healthy body frequency is 62-72 Mhz.) So, what happens when we inhale essential oils? Does our body's frequency rise? In Tanio's frequency experiments the effects of coffee, were measured. It was found that even holding a cup of coffee lowers one's bodily frequency by 8 MHz and that taking a sip can lower one's frequency by 14 MHz. If you are like me and cannot give up coffee, do not panic! The same experiment also shows that when essential oils are inhaled following the exposure to coffee, the bodily frequencies restore themselves in less than a minute, but if no oils are administered, it can take up to three days for the body to recover from even one drink of coffee.

What about prayers? Can prayer raise the oils frequency? Tainio experiments also revealed that the frequencies of oils are also affected by thoughts. Negative thought lowered the frequencies of the oils measured by 12 MHz while positive thoughts raised them by 10 MHz. On the other hand, positive thoughts raised the oils frequencies by 12 MHz. Oils that were prayed over showed even greater increase on its frequency, up to 15 MHz.

IET practitioners can appreciate the connection: We direct the IET energy ray by intent and prayer; essential oils magnify intent; and praying over oils raise their frequency. When we combine energy work and essential oils, and direct them to the area in the body we want to treat, the energy blockages stand no chance. They have to release and come out for healing.

Another fascinating discovery I made in my research is that essential oils were used for healing by priests in ancient times. I found out that in Leviticus 14, which describes a cleansing ceremony performed by the priests for leprosy, a very interesting explanation of how the oils of Cedarwood and Hyssop were used. The priests were to take some oil and anoint the top of the leper's right ear, the right thumb, and the right big toe. Isn't it interesting the choices of these reflex points? Those of you familiar with reflexology probably know that the upper portion of the ear is the trigger point for the releasing emotional issues regarding the mother and father. Fears of the unknown and mental blocks to acquiring wisdom can be released by working the reflex points in the thumb. The big toe is where compulsive behavior can be cleared. What about the choices of Cedarwood and Hyssop for this clearing ceremony? Cedarwood is used in today's aromatherapy to clear emotions of many kinds, but particularly blockages related to the conceit of pride. Hyssop is a releaser of swallowed emotions and spiritual cleanser of past sin. Are we learning something new when we are discovering that our illnesses are connected to our emotions? Probably not! Probably the ancient people understood the underlying emotional basis of degenerative disease and they also knew the emotional release points of the body.

Why are the oils used in this ceremony mentioned in the Bible as well? If they were not important, why would they be there? I like to believe that when the Lord gave this ceremonial direction to Moses, he wanted to make sure that we would have them today: All the information we would need to heal ourselves and others.

There is no doubt in my mind that essential oils play a major role in our effort to release emotional trauma, and may profoundly affect our mood and emotion. Essential oils stimulate the secretion of antibodies, neurotransmitters, endorphins, hormones, and enzymes in the human body. They are as alive as human beings are both, chemically and electrically. It just makes sense to add Essential oils to our healing practice.

Which oil to use for each situation? I have been using different combinations of oils for different situations, and although sometimes, a single essential oil might do the job, I have had best results working with blends.

An essential oil blend can be created for a specific therapeutic effect. A synergistic effect is possible when the essential oils work together harmoniously. You do not need to be an expert in the use of essential oils to create blends. Use your intuition and have fun blending. The following tips will help you to start.

What to consider when creating a blend for emotional release?

1. The purpose of the blend
When blending for the release of specific emotions, look for the

underlined reasons that caused the blockage. Remember to take into account not only the symptoms that you want to treat, but also the underlying causes of the disorder, and the psychological or emotional factors involved. You might consider adding to your blend oils that will work with more than one emotion.

2.   The desired therapeutic effect

Do not blend oils with opposite effects (like a calming and a stimulant). Check thoroughly the properties of the oils that you want to blend and make sure that they complement each other for the particular client you are treating.

3.   The compatibility of the oils

Some essential oils have mutually enhancing powers, while others inhibit each other. Make sure you are choosing oils that work together empowering each other. Oils compatibility is not only important for the therapeutic factor, but also for the scent factor. In my early experiments with blending, I ended with a blend of 9 very scented essential oils that became scentless after been mixed with each other, a blend that although could be work for its purpose, of course, had no application in a therapy called Aroma-therapy.

4.   Make sure your formulation is a balanced blend.

For blending purposes, essential oils are classified into notes. There are four notes classifications. They are the Enhancer notes, Personifier notes, Equalizer notes and Modifier notes. The success of a fragrance composition will depend on how harmoniously balanced these four categories are. It is also important to understand that the order in which the oils are blended is the key to maintaining the desired therapeutic properties in a synergistic blend. If you alter the sequence of adding selected oils to a blend, you may be changing the chemical properties, the fragrance, and consequently, the desired results. In general, oils that are from the same botanical family usually blend well together. In addition, oils that share common constituents also mix well. Start your blend adding the Personifiers first (1-5% of the blend) Personifiers oils have very sharp, strong and long-lasting fragrances. They also have dominant properties with strong therapeutic action. Second add the Enhancers (50-80% of the blend) Enhancer oil should be the predominant oil as it serves to enhance the properties of the other oils in the blend. Its fragrance is mild and is usually of a shorter duration. Third Add the Equalizers (10-15% of the blend) Equalizer oils create balance and synergy among the oils contained in the blend. Their fragrance is also of a shorter duration. Finally, add the Modifier (5-8% of the blend) Modifier oils have a mild and short fragrance. Their function is to add harmony to the blend.

The classification of certain oils is rather complex, which means that many oils have notes in several categories. Certain oils even cover the whole spectrum from top note to base note. For example: ylang-ylang, jasmine or tuberose (with predominance in the Enhancer and base notes), champaca flowers, and rose (with predominance in the top and Enhancer notes). Neroli has most of its notes in the top, but also has a fair amount of Enhancer notes. It is not surprising that such well-balanced oils are the most pleasant that nature has to offer, the most hard to obtain and the most desirable. Obviously, Mother Nature has a profound knowledge fragrance classification.

At a glance, the science of blending might sound rather complicated, but do not become discouraged, as you become familiar with the essential oils, you will find that blending is a very pleasurable experience. Start small, blending 3 or 4 oils in the beginning. Use your imagination and intuition as you progress. You will want to familiarize yourself with the fragrance and effect of essential oils. Breathe the aroma and note how it makes you feel - calm, uplifted, focused, energized? Is the scent light, fresh, strong, sweet? Does this scent bring any emotion into your mind?

If you feel that blending is something that you will enjoy doing and want to learn more, I highly recommend that you get the book Aromatherapy Workbook by Marcel Lavabre. This book is a perfect step-by-step guide for beginners as well as an ongoing reference for practicing aromatherapy.

The following list provides you with information on some of the essential oils traditionally used for emotional healing. You will notice that several oils can be used to treat the same emotion, as an example, to release fear you can use: Basil, Frankincense, Nutmeg, Thyme and Black Pepper. To release worthlessness, you can use Frankincense, Neroli, Sandalwood. The oils versatility will give you plenty of room to play with the notes, desired therapeutic effects and compatibility of the oils to create a well-balanced blend.

ESSENTIAL OILS TRADITIONALLY USED FOR EMOTIONAL HEALING

Angelica – *angelica archangelica*

The fragrance named after the angels can assist us in times we feel uncertain about our spirituality, spiritually neglected and need to call upon the angels to give us understanding and open the pathway for us. Although extremely powerful by itself, it seems to be more effective when blended with other fragrances as it is in this synergy. It grounds and connects us with angelic guidance. Blending classification = Personifier, Modifier

Basil (Sweet) - *Ocimum basilicum*

Basil assists in awakening; awareness; and understanding. It allows the clearance of a muddled mind that puts up a barrier to contacting angels. Basil balances the 6th chakra. Basil is widely used to treat: Addiction, Drugs related Anxiety, Apathy, Confusion Dementia, Doubt, mental & intellectual fatigue, Fear of failure, Fear in general, Hypochondria, lack of memory, Rejection and Memory loss. Blending classification = Enhancer and Equalizer.

Bergamot - *citrus bergamia*

Bergamot can help to lift the fog that separates us from the source. It helps us to see clear God's divine direction for us. It encourages confidence, balance and joy.

Blending classification = Equalizer, Modifier and Enhancer.

Birch - *betula alleghaniensis*

Birch is the fragrance to use in a sacred space, before using a more spiritually connecting fragrance it is the celestial cleanser that sweeps away the misdirected and misguided forms. Blending classification = Personifier and Enhancer.

Black Pepper - *piper nigrum*

Black Pepper is a protective fragrance that, when used with the right intent and purpose, allows our guardian angels to bring protective elements into our lives. It can also help us when we are fearful of reuniting ourselves with spiritual aspects of life after long-term neglect. It is a balancer for the first chackra. Blending classification = Enhancer

Cedarwood – *cedrus atlantica*

It brings in positive energy. Balances the first chakra and releases anxiety. It also encourages focus, balance, concentration and brings the energy of the angels of wisdom closer for purification. Cedarwood grounds, promote strengths and confidence. Cedarwood Is mentioned in the bible 11 times. It was used traditionally by the North American Indians to enhance their potential for spiritual communications. Blending classification = Enhancer and Equalizer

Clary Sage - *salvia sclarea*

Clary Sage is wonderful at times when we pray for assistance from the angels, to reveal our purpose, or at least understand a little the reason for our struggles. It supports us in pursuing our dreams, if we are the only one to believe it will come true. It aids in releasing the blockages of guilt. Gently awakens the angelic realm of the subconscious, bringing harmony and purpose. Blending classification = Personifier.

Fennel - *foeniculum vulgare*

Fennel is wonderful in aiding us in keeping the mind stable and functional, yet uplifted. To remain grounded, and to help understand the lessons we are meant to learn in this lifetime. In the ancient Egypt and Roman, fennel was believed to bestow strength, courage and longevity. Blending Classification: Equalizer and Modifier

Frankincense – *boswellia carteri*

Frankincense is adaptogenic – It will adapt to a person's spiritual state of being, offering support in a wide range of circumstances. It induces the feelings of emotional stability, enlightenment and inspiration. Frankincense grounds; calms, promotes meditative states. Frankincense is one of the most frequently mentioned healing oils of the Bible. There are at least 22 direct references to frankincense by name. Frankincense helps to release fear of change, fear of letting go. Also, releases our feelings of worthlessness. Induce feelings of emotional stability and inspiration. Frankincense balances the 7th chakra. Blending Classification = Enhancer & Equalizer.

Galbanum - *ferula galbaniflua*

Galbanum is the fragrance that allows for the shedding of old ideas and outdated behavior and attitudes. It promotes the total surrender to the creator. Galbanum was Biblical medicine. It is one of the ingredients for holy incense. Holy incense is mentioned 54 times in the scriptures, which are the equivalent 54 mentions of galbanum in the bible. It is used to increase spiritual awareness and meditative state. Blending Classification = Enhancer & Equalizer

Geranium - *pelargonium graveolens*

Geranium brings in the feeling of being soothed, protected and mothered. It provides comfort and reassurance by bringing the angelic realms close to us. It helps in the release of negative memories and takes us back to a place of joy and peace. Blending Classification = Enhancer & Equalizer

Grapefruit – *citrus paradisi*

Grapefruit disperses emotional energy blockages, promotes confidence and increases intuition. It energizes the subconscious connections and clears the pathway to direct connection to the angelic realm. It helps us to release negativity. Blending classification = Modifier & Enhancer.

Helychrysum - *helicrysum italicum*; promotes persistence, endurance, and courage and enables the path ahead to be clearer, full of awareness of perhaps the dangers and pitfalls of life. It helps us to understand that to love truly involves the acceptance of the pain of love. It cannot heal the past nor protect the heart from future hurt, but it does make self-exposure safe. It brings in the energy of trust in the universe. Blending classification = Personifier.

Hyssop - *hyssopus officinalis*

Hyssop is the fragrance that connects us to the realms of divine wisdom. It purifies and cleanses, promotes tolerance and understanding and unconditional love. Hyssop promotes clarity of spirit, equilibrium, trust and faith. For the removal of emotional uncleanness, assistance in the expansion of the protective beings, but very much on the physical plane, assists in the removal of the heritage of guilt and fear miasmas of a psychological nature. Purifying for those who believe they have sins that must be forgiven. The scent of Hyssop is a spiritual cleanser of sin & immorality. Hyssop encourages awakening closed hearts and minds. Hyssop promotes divine direction, clarity and harmony. Hyssop promotes calm, forgiveness, equilibrium, truth and faith. Hyssop is a releaser of swallowed emotions. Hyssop is mentioned in the bible 12 times. Blending classification = Enhancer, Equalizer and Modifier.

Jasmine - *jasminum grandiflorum*

Jasmine inspires, promotes love, creativity and intuition. It is the fragrance of the shinning enlightened ones for when we need to call on them for assistance in getting a clear picture of our life purpose. In many religious traditions, the jasmine flower symbolizes hope, happiness and love. Jasmine uplifts the emotions, increases intuitive states and wisdom. Blending classification = Equalizer, Modifier & Enhancer.

Juniper Berry - *juniperus communis*

Juniper protects against negativity and disperses energy blockages. It is very effective in controlling addictions. It provides assistance during purification, when we lower our protective barrier and feel our energy drained. It can be used during meditation to help bring the beings of light into the setting, and to understand why negative experiences may he troubling us. Juniper is mentioned in the Bible 4 times. Juniper evokes feelings of health, love and peace. It was used by various American Indian groups for purification. It is used in Tibet in ritual incense. Juniper encourages enlightenment and humility. Blending classification: Equalizer

Lavender - *lavendula officinalis*

Is useful in all energy treatments to relax and balance. Lavender embodies the warm, protective love of Mother Earth. It brings in the positive energy that allows us to feel safe and cared for. It is useful in all energy treatments to relax and balance. Lavender brings in positive energy, awakens harmony. It's a vibration that brings the angels of compassion closer when we are in need of comfort and companionship and recognition that help is always available to us, and that we aren't ever alone. Lavender induces peace and dispels depression. It calms stormy or uncontrolled emotional states. Lavender is very active in the auric field. It is cherishing and nurturing. It encourages forgiveness, acceptance & reconciliation. Lavender lifts the weight of sadness that sometimes covers our spirit. Blending classification = Enhancer, Modifier & Equalizer.

Lemongrass - *Cymbopogon flexuosus*

The sweet fragrance of lemongrass is a wonderful aid to trigger memories related to child abuse. Sometimes these memories are so deeply buried that they do not manifest themselves until early-to-mid-adult. Lemongrass is widely used for spiritual purification and to promote psychic awareness. It clears regrets or shame and gives us the clarity to see that the choice has always been ours. Blending classification = Enhancer & Equalizer.

Mandarin – *citrus reticulata*

Mandarin assists us in reconnecting with our inner child by bringing back briefly the innocence of childhood prayers. It brings tranquility and facilitates the connection with the high realms. It helps to control stress and irritability. Blending classification = Personifier & Modifier.

Marjoram – *thymus mastschina*

Marjoram can be used to help to assist us when we become obsessive, or when we find it hard to release persistent mental anguish. It balances the first chakra encouraging calm, balance, perseverance and sincerity. We may think of Marjoram as a good friend that would tell us, speak not of evil or be judgmental. Try instead to forgive without judgment or criticism to maintain a clear and untroubled heart. Marjoram is also excellent to support the release of deep emotional trauma, (grief, loneliness, etc.). It promotes peace and Sleep. Marjoram aids on achieving high consciousness during meditation. Blending classification: Enhancer and Equalizer

Myrrh - *commiphora myrrha*

Myrrh is very effective in supporting our spiritual journeys. Its grounding properties allow us to be secure at the same time we reinforce our spiritual connections. Myrrh links us with the pathway of our soul. It gives us the feeling of protection by trusting our inner feelings. Myrrh is directly referred in the bible 40 times. Used with intent, Myrrh's fragrance enables us to let go of the need to battle for the just, against the unjust. It reminds us that everything that God does or allows to happen is perfect even if at a time we do not comprehend. Blending classification = Modifier & Equalizer.

Nutmeg - *myristica fragrans*

Nutmeg brings the dreams of angelic realms into conscious thought. It promotes the release of fear, especially in times of changes. The fragrance of nutmeg encourages calm, peace, visions, dreams and stillness. It encourages us to find our true selves and exercise our self-expression. It allows the spirit to soar. The fragrance of nutmeg has been used in ritual where the intent is prosperity. Taking this inconsideration, Nutmeg may also be helpful in manifesting meditation. Blending classification = Personifier.

Neroli – *citrus Aurantium*

Neroli is known as one of the fragrances of the angelic realms. Using Neroli with prayers and intent might allow you to feel the soothing brush of angel's wings. Neroli's high vibration brings in positive energy and stabilizes the 2nd and 4th chakras. It promotes communication with the spiritual world and with mankind. It helps to dissipate our feelings of worthlessness. Neroli is not considered an aphrodisiac, but it calms the conscious mind, dispels worries over sexual performance and can smooth the path to mutually satisfying sexual relations. Blending classification = Equalizer, Modifier and Personifier.

Orange - *citrus sinensis*

Aids in releasing blockages of Self-blame, Withdrawal from life. It brings the joy of our assigned angels into our hearts, to be touched with happiness that remains within us always, if we can only acknowledge it. In the ancient time, orange was associated with generosity, gratitude and innocence. It encourages joy, creativity and self-confidence. Blending classification = Enhancer & Personifier.

Palmorosa – *cymbopogon martinii*

Palmorosa helps all levels of healing and develops wisdom. Palmarosa reminds us that what lies in the domain of our mind becomes a reality in our life. That traveling the road of an illuminated heart we can overcome impediments of the physical world and let our spirit soar. Palmorosa brings the feeling of security, reduces stress, calms the mind and clear the thoughts. Blending classification = Enhancer & Equalizer.

Patchouli - *popostemon cablin*

It aids in the release of fear of taking chances in the direction of our dreams. Patchouli is the fragrance of action that reminds us that for our ideal to occur, we must take actions. The scent of Patchouli is useful in rising sexual desire. With proper visualization, it releases anxiety regarding sex and intimacy. Its vibration is synchronized with money and abundance, making patchouli an excellent choice in manifesting work. Patchouli eases anxiety. Blending classification: Enhancer

Peppermint - *mentha piperita*

Peppermint is the fragrance that promotes healthy self-esteem and clarity in communication. Inspires and opens up our creativity. The ancients Romans used Peppermint to rouse the conscious mind. Peppermint is powerful for this purpose. It encourages self-acceptance, It stimulates the dreams stage and allows us to bring from our dreams information and understanding to apply in our conscious life. Blending classification = Personifier

Petitgrain - *citrus aurantium*

Petitgrain frequency provides us with a gentle awakening of our consciousness and connects, if only briefly, with the subconscious and higher self, aligning our conscious mind with the desires of our hearts. It encourages self-confidence and expressiveness. It helps us in building spiritual bridges between us and other people that are meant to support our soul mission. When we are feeling fragile and vulnerable to the opinion of others, we need the stability and the gentle spiritual strength provided by Petitgrain. It wakes us to find strength in our personal truth. Through our personal truth and the gentle awakening promoted by Petitgrain, we can connect, spiritually attuning with spiritual growth. Blending classification = Enhancer, Modifier & Personifier.

Rosemary - *rosmarinus officinalis*

Rosemary encourages confidence. It helps us to remember who we are and what our place is on this planet. It gives us the confidence to stop worshiping the opinion of others and exercise our free will. Rosemary stimulates memory, energizes the solar plexus and opens the conscious mind. Blending classification = Enhancer

Rose – *rosa damascena*

To inhale the fragrance of rose is like inhaling the sweet love and hug of an angel. It promotes creativity, love, compassion, joy. It is associated with the desires of the human heart. Rose promotes creativity, love compassion and sense of wellbeing. The vibration of Rose resonates with the vibration of unconditional love; it eases the sorrow and brings comfort and joy to the heart and soul. Blending classification = Personifier, Enhancer, Equalizer and Modifier.

Rosewood - *aniba rosaeodora*

Rosewood is the fragrance that opens us to spirituality. It brings in positive energy and disperses energy blockages, especially blockages of shame. Rosewood balances the 5th chakra. Blending classification: Modifier & Equalizer

Sandalwood - *santalum album*

Sandalwood quiets the mind. It promotes states of higher consciousness, facilitating deep meditation states. It assists us in the joining of the physical and spiritual realms. Sandalwood calms and comforts. To release our feeling of worthlessness, sandalwood comes to our rescue. It is the fragrance that supports us while we give permission to ourselves to be the driver of our life. It helps in third eye opening. It calms and balances emotions. Blending classification = Modifier & Equalizer

Spikenard – *nardastachus jatamansi*

Spikenard comforts the heart, increases spiritual pride and spiritual love. It brings close to us the angels of potentiality. It expands our contracts, revealing the secrets of the soul and the light of the universe. Its purpose is to release us from the chains of our past action, which persistently blind us to repeating actions that affect the freedom of the spirit. Spikenard is mentioned in the bible 17 times.

Spruce –*picea mariana*

Spruce is high in monoterpene. Monoterpene has the ability to reprogram miswritten information in the cellular memory. Spruce balances the 5th chakra and promotes clear communications of inner feelings. Spruce Helps to release emotional blockages. Blending classification = Equalizer & Enhancer.

Thyme - *thymus vulgaris*

Clears energy blockages and relieves fear. It promotes self-confidence and release trauma. The fragrance of thyme can come to our rescue when there is a need for reconciliation and compassion. It facilitates tolerance and courage. Blending classification = Equalizer & Enhancer.

Ylang Ylang - *cananga odorata*

Ylang Ylang helps to release self-blame at the same time calms and sooths our trouble minds allowing us to have joy, peace and confidence in the steps we must take for the realization of our dreams. Ylang Ylang promotes courage and self-confidence. It opens our hearts to gratitude. It supports us in exercising our creativity. It helps to release frustration, irritability and impatience. It calms anger and all negative emotional states; it transforms negative energy into more positive manifestation. It is exceptionally helpful in overcoming emotional sexual problems. Blending classification = Personifier & Modifier.

Note: It requires about 1,000 pounds of Jasmine (about 3.6 million) fresh unpicked blossoms) to yield one pound of jasmine oil. The blossoms must be collected before sunrise, or the fragrance will be evaporated. No wonder a single pound of therapeutic jasmine oil can cost from $1,200.00 to $4,500.00.

Now you have enough information to start making your own blends, but remember, for therapeutic results you need to work with therapeutic essential oils. Adulteration of essential oils is becoming more and more common these days. As the demand for them increases and their availability decreases, the temptation to thin the oils with solvents is great. Export and Import charts, shows that Frankincense for example, was been exported in quantities 100 times higher than it was produced.

For you to get the expected results you need, therapeutic essential oils of the highest quality are needed. Important criteria to consider when selecting essential oils include the following: 100% therapeutic and natural, country of origin, extraction method (e.g., distillation, expression), part of the plant used and most importantly the reputation of the company providing the oils. You need to know and trust your source and also make sure that your source knows and trusts their source. Many vendors are not aware that the oils they buy and sell have been diluted, or worse yet, come from chemical laboratories. Presently, there is no agency responsible for certifying that an essential oil is therapeutic grade. There is no requirement that ingredients be listed on essential oils bottles. This gives the unscrupulous manufacturers the opportunity to make any claim they want. Inquire in your area for a good supplier, but keep in mind that therapeutic, therapeutic essential oils, normally are not sold in retail stores.

Also, you might consider experimenting with prepared blends. Several companies offer a wide range of blends. The best way to get acquainted with those blends is searching the internet. Two good sources to begin your search are Young Living (www.Youngliving.com) and Caroline Myss (www.myss.com) web sites. Those two sources provide oils for a wide range of emotions and might be just what you need.

With the guidance of the 9 healing angels I work with, I have formulated 10 essential oils blends for emotional release, specifically to use with Integrated Energy Therapy®. The oils were chosen carefully, considering their electrical frequency, vibration, their compatibility with each other, and especially their compatibility with the cellular memory anatomy. Also, they were chosen considering their correlation with the specific emotions being treated. Although these blends were formulated primarily to be used with Integrated Energy Therapy®, they work very well with any other energy work technique and even for any personal needs to release a specific emotion. For information on those blends please email: Arielavb@aol.com. And live your phone number for a call back.

ABOUT THE AUTHOR

Antonia (Toni) Brasted is a Doctor of Philosophy (Ph.D.) in Holistic Counseling, an Interfaith Minister with a Master Degree in Metaphysics from University of Metaphysics, a Certified Grief Counselor, a Registered Aromatherapist and a Master Instructor for Integrated energy Therapy.

Brazilian born, Antonia emigrated to The United States, leaving behind 18 years of study and practice in spirituality. During the last 34 years she has studied Aromatheraphy, Herbalogy, Ayurveda, Chakra Alignment, Color Therapy, Sound Healing, Energy Healing, Light Body Development and Energy Medicine.

She is a Pastoral/Spiritual Counselor and she works as a Chaplain/ Grief Counselor for Hospices in Nevada for more than 20 years, providing spiritual care for terminally ill patients and families. Through bereavement support, she has helped many to go through their grief and find new meaning for life.

She is a certified practitioner and master instructor of Integrated Energy Therapy. IET® - Developed by Stevan Thayer the founder of the Center of Being. Integrated Energy Therapy ® is a gentle yet powerful, hand on energy therapy that gets your issues out of your tissues.

She is an intuitive channeler. With her guide Angel Ariel, she has helped many to see a clear picture of their lives, through energy healing and spiritual counseling, resolving their fears, frustrations and struggles.

She believes that as souls, we all have important missions to accomplish in this lifetime. When we discover what our life purpose is (and accomplish it) we will end our struggle, we will be filled with joy. Everything in our life will start working for our highest good. She claims that the most effective way to access one's inner wisdom (the wisdom of the soul) is daily meditation. With the regular practice of meditation, sooner or later you will tap into that hidden knowledge and will learn not only what your life-purpose is, but also the real reason for many of your struggles: Knowledge brings wisdom.

SERVICES THE AUTHOR PROVIDES
INTEGRATED ENERGY THERAPY ® - IET

IET is a highly effective and gentle healing technique. Cellular memory in our physical and energetic bodies store memories of our feelings such as suppressed traumas, fears, emotions, and limiting beliefs. Over time, these memories can affect our energy level, health, and general well-being. IET safely supports you and helps to release these negative emotions while replacing them with positive emotions.

No matter where you live in the world, you can receive the full benefits of IET in the comfort and convenience of your own home. Energy has no boundaries and it is guided by our intention. Absentee session – Includes pre-session phone call to discuss the client needs and post session phone call review.

INTEGRATED ENERGY THERAPY ® - IET

Training Classes

Integrated Energy Therapy' is ideal for students wanting to begin an energy therapy practice, and also provides a wonderful complement to other holistic techniques such as Massage, Reiki, and Therapeutic Touch. While IET is a perfect standalone energy therapy system; it is also ideal to integrate IET into sessions based on other holistic modalities, as well as integrate the techniques of other holistic modalities into IET sessions

Due to the nature of the Integrated Energy Therapy Training which requires attunements to be carried out in person the classes are taught in person only. Presently, the classes are held in Las Vegas only. You can learn the Basic, Intermediate and, Advanced levels of Integrated Energy Therapy® in 3 days. (Each level = 8 hours training day). You might consider traveling to Las Vegas for a 3 day learning vacation. Classes are limited to 6 students. Consider sponsoring the classes - If you bring 5 friends to take the classes with you, your classes will be **FREE**.

GRIEFCOUSELING/SPIRITUALCOUNSELING

Are you feeling "stuck"? Sometimes a problem seems to stay put, and it feels like it will be there forever. Are you experiencing one of these symptoms?

- Depressed, irritable mood,
- Feeling guilty or worthlessness,
- Difficulty concentrating,
- Inability to relate to others,
- Loss of interest in activities,
- Feeling panicky, financial stress,
- Relationship issues,
- Recent loss,
- Trauma.

Intuitive Pastoral/Spiritual Counseling, combined with energy healing, can assist you in releasing the draining emotional, mental and karmic patterns from your life. Our physical body is a reflection of our inner being. Symptoms as those mentioned above, are most likely triggered by blockages in our energy body. Energy blockages in the human body are caused by physical trauma, surgery, disease, emotional crisis, suppressed feelings, stress, fear, self-limiting thoughts and karma. They limit our experience of life and can result in energy depletion, lack of enthusiasm for life, and even disease.

For more information or to make an appointment, for any of the services listed here, please email: Arielavb@aol.com with your name, phone number and questions you may have, I will call you back as soon as possible.

"All consultations are kept in the utmost confidentiality."

BIBLIOGRAPHY

Ambroise-Auguste Liebeault - https://en.wikipedia.org/wiki/ Ambroise-Auguste Liébeault

Barbara Brennan – Hands of light – 1993

Benson, Herbert - The Relaxation Response Mass Market – 1976

Becker, M.D. Robert - Body Electric: Electromagnetism and the Foundation of life - 1998

Becker, MD, Robert - Electromagnetic Healing | Subtle Energy - https://subtle.energy/life- fields-and-the- power- of- regeneration

Bradford, Michael - The Healing Energy of Your Hands - 1996

Bruce Tainio - Bruce and Tainio Technology Wave Quantum https://wavequantumblog.uk/2021/02/03/brucetanio

Caroline Myss - Anatomy of the Spirit – 1996

Count Wilhelm Von Reichenbach - https://www.findagrave.com/memorial/135249726/wilhelm-von_reichenbach

Dejan Rakovic & Gordana Vitaliano - http://www.vsm.com/21R.7.html and http://www.vsm.com/21R.36.html

De La Warr, George - https://en.wikipedia.org › wiki › George_de_la_Warr

Drown, Ruth - Guidot - Radionic / Psychotronic Photography: G. De La Warr, Ruth Drown (rexresearch.com)

Duane Packer and Sanaya Roman - Developing your Light Body - http://www.orindaben.com

Dolores Krieger Ph.D. R.N - Therapeutic Touch Inner workbook-1996

Dossey, Larry - Careful What You Pray For...You Just Might Get it! (1998)

Frank, E.Wilson - Faith and practice - 1992

Franz Mesmer - https://en.wikipedia. org/wiki/Franz_Mesmer

Fruits and Premature Aging - https://younglife.org

Gaston Naessens - Naessens somatid theory - https://www.faim.org/gaston-nacssens-and-714x

Gawain, Shakti - The Four Levels of Healing: A Guide to Balancing the Spiritual, Mental, Emotional, and Physical Aspects of Life (Gawain, Shakti) Paperback – 1999

Herz, Dr. Rachel Sarah - https://rachelherz.com/

International Society for the Study of Subtle Energies and Energy Medicine - https://www.issseemscience.org

Kilner,Walter - https://en.wikipedia.org/wiki/Walter_John_Kilner

Kirlian Semyon - https://en.wikipedia.org › wiki › Kirlian_ photography

Mother Teresa of Calcutta - htm http://www.preach-the- gospel.com/Its-between-you- and-God.htm

Motoyama, Hiroshi – https://en.wikipedia.org › wiki › Hiroshi _Motoyama

Naessens, Gustave - https://www.faim.org/gaston- naessens-and- 714x

Pierrakas,John and Eva - https://https://en.wikipedia.org/wiki/John_Pierrakos

Qigong: Benefits, types, side effects, and more - https://www.medicalnewstoday.com/articles/qigon g-benefits

Rand William - www.reiki.org/users/william-rand

Reichenbach, Baron Carl von - The Concept of Odic Force - https://psy-minds.com

Robins M.D.,Eric - http://www.pranichealinguk.com/Doctors.htm#robns

Royal Raymond Rife - https://www.bing.com/ search?q=royal+raymond+rife

Semmelweis,Ignaz - https://en.wikipedia.org › wiki › Ignaz_Semmelweis

Shakespeare - w.w.w. Shakespeare's Richard II: Reflections on the Undoing of a King.

Shen Nong's - Miracle - Herbs – 2005

Sutherland, MD Willian – Cranial Sacral Therapy History/1 (craniosacral-online.co.uk) – http://www.craniosacraltherapy

Thayer, Stevan J. Thayer - https://www.learniet.com

The Olfactory Tract - New Atlas of Human Anatomy (1999 Barnes & Noble's book)

Usui, MD.,Mikao - Ascension Reiki - www.ascensionreiki.com/Dr.-Mikao- Usui.html

Valerie Hunt, MD- The Human Energy Field: Dr. Valerie Hunt Interview (Part 1) | Awaken – https://awaken.com/2021/11/the-human- energy-field

Valnet Ann M.D. -The Practice of Aromatherapy - 1982

Van Helmont - https://www.researchgate.net/Publication/264038630_Van_Helmont

Wang Yang Guang – Yang Guang Biography: Emperor Yang of Sui (569 - 618 AD) (totallyhistory.com)

Wilhelm Reich - https://en.wikipedia.org › wiki › Wilhelm Reich

Wilson, Frank F.   Faith and practice by Wilson, Frank E. - Randon House, 1939

Zheng Ronliang - Lanzhou University, Lanzhou | LZU - https://www.researchgate.net/profile/Rongliang- Zheng

Zeigler Patrick - https://reikijohn.com/history/patrick-zieglers- story/

Young Life Research Clinic (YLRC) - young life research clinic - institute of natural medicine - utah company (utah-biz.com)

Printed in the United States
by Baker & Taylor Publisher Services